DAVID PREECE

SECONDARY GEOGRAPHY IN ACTION

IN ACTION SERIES

A **WALKTHRUs** PRODUCTION

Together we unlock every learner's unique potential

At Hachette Learning (formerly Hodder Education), there's one thing we're certain about. No two students learn the same way. That's why our approach to teaching begins by recognising the needs of individuals first.

Our mission is to allow every learner to fulfil their unique potential by empowering those who teach them. From our expert teaching and learning resources to our digital educational tools that make learning easier and more accessible for all, we provide solutions designed to maximise the impact of learning for every teacher, parent and student.

Aligned to our parent company, Hachette Livre, founded in 1826, we pride ourselves on being a learning solutions provider with a global footprint.

www.hachettelearning.com

Although every effort has been made to ensure that website addresses are correct at time of going to press, Hachette Learning cannot be held responsible for the content of any website mentioned in this book. It is sometimes possible to find a relocated web page by typing in the address of the home page for a website in the URL window of your browser.

Hachette UK's policy is to use papers that are natural, renewable and recyclable products and made from wood grown in well-managed forests and other controlled sources. The logging and manufacturing processes are expected to conform to the environmental regulations of the country of origin.

To order, please visit www.HachetteLearning.com or contact Customer Service at education@hachette.co.uk / +44 (0)1235 827827.

ISBN: 978 1 9152 6187 8

© David Preece 2025

First published in 2025 by
Hachette Learning,
An Hachette UK Company
Carmelite House
50 Victoria Embankment
London EC4Y 0DZ
www.HachetteLearning.com

The authorised representative in the EEA is Hachette Ireland, 8 Castlecourt Centre, Dublin 15, D15 XTP3, Ireland (email: info@hbgi.ie)

Impression number   10 9 8 7 6 5 4 3 2 1
Year   2029 2028 2027 2026 2025

All rights reserved. Apart from any use permitted under UK copyright law, no part of this publication may be reproduced or transmitted in any form or by any means, electronic or mechanical, including photocopying and recording, or held within any information storage and retrieval system, without permission in writing from the publisher or under licence from the Copyright Licensing Agency Limited. Further details of such licences (for reprographic reproduction) may be obtained from the Copyright Licensing Agency Limited, www.cla.co.uk

Cover illustration by Oliver Caviglioli
Illustrations by DC Graphic Design Limited, Hextable, Kent.
Typeset in the UK.
Printed in the UK.

A catalogue record for this title is available from the British Library.

To Marianne, Mom, Dad & Richard –
you have always been the most important things in my world.

To the memory of Robin Austin,
one of the finest teachers and people I have ever known.

CONTENTS

Acknowledgements vi

Series foreword viii

About the author xii

Chapter 1 How do we put geography into action? 1

Chapter 2 How do we approach the discipline of geography? 8

Chapter 3 What are the debates and perspectives in the subject community? ... 27

Chapter 4 How do we sequence a geography curriculum? 34

Chapter 5 Whose geographies do we teach? 39

Chapter 6 How do we create challenge in the geography classroom? 63

Chapter 7 How do we plan great geography lessons? 73

Chapter 8 How do we inspire awe and wonder in the geography classroom? ... 91

Chapter 9 How do we teach geographical skills in the classroom? 98

Chapter 10 How do we assess progress in the geography curriculum? 114

Chapter 11 How do we take geography outside the classroom? 134

Chapter 12 How do we take geography beyond the curriculum? 152

Chapter 13 How do we support students to choose geography? 158

References and further reading 169

ACKNOWLEDGEMENTS

Throughout my teaching career – and now, as I work with trainees, and therefore say so often that they're probably sick of it – I continually reinforce the idea that teaching is a team sport. I've never believed that anyone could do this alone. The mistakes I've made are mine, but the best of this book, and of my teaching, is a distillation of all of the kindness, subject expertise and teaching experience that I've been fortunate to acquire through osmosis from the many talented people I have worked with.

Thank you to Keith Phipps, Chris Jackson and Mike Roden for inspiring me to study geography in the first place, and making sure I had the chance to explore a world which I never thought would be open to me.

I am privileged to have worked with amazing geography teachers who taught me so much about how to make this subject come alive. Thank you to Christopher Ruck, Dave Lawson, Emily Partridge, John Snelling, Liz Morris, Mike Alexander, Peter Dawson, Rachael Biggs, Rebecca Wallace, Rob Brookman and Sam Powell – for memories, lessons, field trips and friendships that have lasted beyond the classroom and marking discussions!

Of course, I've also been inspired and grateful for teachers who have made my professional and pastoral career so much better, even though they weren't geographers. My thanks to David Sharples, Debbie Warren, Fiona Linfield, Gareth Stewart, Gemma & Richard Davies, Hilary Baptiste, Jenny McCloskey, Joe McKee, John & Fran Short-Ring, Tim Hofmeyr, Roxy Butryn, Richard and Sarah Preece – who taught me more about primary than I could have hoped! – and the wonderful and brilliant schoolmaster Robin Austin.

As I have moved into the wider world of teacher education, I have been hugely fortunate to work with and learn from some incredibly wise geographers and wider educational thinkers. Thank you to Alistair Hamill, Ben Davey, Cat Batch, Claire Brown, Darren Bailey, David Gardner, Emma King, Dr Emma Rawlings Smith, Helen Webb, Iram Sammar, Jessica Burger, Karen Corfield, Lin Goram, Mark Enser, Nicola Farley, Rachel Arthur, Rosie Clark, Sarah Ross, Stefan Carron and Vicki Poutney, who have made this journey so enjoyable, and taught me so much about so many different aspects of education.

I am hugely grateful to my students, trainees, and the people who shared their wisdom, and generously wrote case studies for this book. Thank you to Abdurrahman Perez-McMillan, Alice Moy, Brendan Conway, Chloe Searl, Clare Proctor, George Zarkos, Graeme Schofield, Joseph Milton, Kelly Daish, Kit-Marie Rackley, Sadie Pither and Sinem Ishlek for trusting me with the privilege of sharing your stories.

Thank you to Tom Sherrington, for having the idea for this book, and giving me the chance to write it. Finally, this book would not exist without the expert wisdom and editing skill of Catherine Fitzsimons, who took my jumble of ideas and turned them in to something that you could read.

The author and publishers would like to thank the Geographical Association for permission to reproduce copyright material.

SERIES FOREWORD

This series of books was commissioned as a WalkThrus Production to complement two of our other series: The *Teaching Walkthrus*, Volumes 1, 2 and 3, and the *In Action* series. We believe that, together, they represent a powerful resource for teachers in schools and colleges in multiple subject settings.

The *In Action* series has proven to be very popular with busy teachers, enabling them to engage with a range of important ideas from cognitive science and from education research more generally. In each book, the authors explore the key ideas from a specific researcher, translating them into practical approaches that teachers can adopt in their practice. So far, the series includes:

- Rosenshine's Principles of Instruction
- Collins et al's Cognitive Apprenticeship
- Fiorella & Mayer's Generative Learning
- Shimamura's MARGE Model of Learning
- Sweller's Cognitive Load Theory
- Wiliam & Leahy's Five Formative Assessment Strategies
- Annie Murphy Paul's The Extended Mind
- Dunlosky's Strengthening the Student Toolbox
- Berger's An Ethic of Excellence
- Bjork & Bjork's Desirable Difficulties
- Ausubel's Meaningful Learning

Each of these books is a guide to interpreting the research in ways that can be applied in real-world classrooms. We have been delighted by the response to the series, with teachers telling us they value the brevity and clarity and the examples of theory in practice. It's so important for teachers to have a good grounding in cognitive science so that they have not only a clear model of how learning happens but also an understanding of all the potential barriers or difficulties that students experience. Bridging the gap between research and practice is a significant challenge because real-world classrooms are so much more complicated than the controlled conditions usually set up to investigate specific concepts in trials. The authors of the *In Action* books are all serving teachers or have taught in schools for many years, so their take on the theories and concepts that their books focus on is important and incredibly useful, grounded in the reality of teaching whole, complex classes.

It's by no means a comprehensive list – not yet – and we recognise that many other aspects of research would benefit from the same treatment. Books on Nuthall's Hidden Lives of Learners, Engelmann's ideas on direct instruction and Bandura's ideas on self-efficacy are all in the pipeline. We would also encourage every teacher to engage with Dan Willingham's *Why Don't Students Like School?*.

Released in parallel with the research-informed *In Action* series, our *Teaching WalkThrus* have also been popular with over 350,000 copies distributed across the three volumes. The idea of breaking ideas down into five-step visual guides, with short punchy descriptions, has proven very successful, allowing teachers to engage with a broad range of ideas in a very accessible format that informs their training, coaching or personal reflection. Significantly, *Teaching WalkThrus* were written in a style that is context free. They are generic in style so that teachers of all subjects in any setting can engage with them, transposing the ideas into their real-world contexts. The 150+ WalkThrus are organised into six main series, each of which represents an important area for professional learning:

Behaviour and relationships
- Lesson management
- Planning for good behaviour
- Positive correction
- Relationships and mindsets

Curriculum planning
- Assessment issues
- Broad design concepts
- Challenge, inclusion, diversity
- Detailed planning

Explaining and modelling
- Giving explanations and modelling
- Reading and writing

- Standards, expectations and scaffolding
- Types of explanations

Questioning and feedback
- Assessment
- Core questioning techniques
- Deeper questioning techniques
- Feedback

Practice and retrieval
- Guided to independent practice
- Reading
- Building fluency
- Retrieval practice
- Support and challenge

Mode B teaching
- Choices and creativity
- Making it real
- Oracy
- Student directed activities

With over 4000 schools having engaged with our online WalkThrus toolkit, we know that a great deal of valuable professional learning can be supported with our generic guides as a starting point. However, throughout each book we are at pains to stress the crucial need to adapt the ideas for specific circumstances. A five-step visual WalkThrus guide is not a set of rigid rules – it is a framework for thinking through an idea, deconstructing it so that teachers can then reconstruct it themselves, forming their own mental models for enacting powerful techniques in their own classrooms. That's the spirit.

Now, having explored research ideas in the *In Action* series and general pedagogical ideas in WalkThrus, we felt that the logical next step was to bring in subject-specific books in this new series, completing the third pillar of the trio: research, pedagogy, curriculum. Each book in the *In Action* subject series has been written by practising teachers who were tasked with presenting a summary of important ideas and debates from their subject to support busy teachers in their work. We have not imposed a rigid common format and our authors were encouraged to share their own perspectives with our readers. There is no definitive book on teaching science or history or maths or physical education – so these books are explicitly written with that in mind. The books represent the authors' personal perspective on how the ideas that circulate within each subject community can translate into great practice in the classroom. Once again, we invite readers to then adapt and adopt the ideas that make sense in their context.

I have to congratulate each author on their excellent work. It's daunting to summarise and capture the spirit of a subject, balancing depth of detail with sufficient breadth of coverage of content and related debates and implementation issues – all in what is meant to be a short book. If there is one thing that characterises all our books it is that they are accessible to teachers who are time poor. Each book in this series achieves that goal – they have an energy to them and a brilliant balance of rigour, steeped in experience with teaching the subject, alongside tons of examples to bring things to life.

We hope you find this book interesting and useful, adding an important dimension to your wider reading as a teacher doing the most important work there is: developing young people so that they have the knowledge, experience, confidence and wisdom they need to make sense of their world and play their part in the communities they belong to.

ABOUT THE AUTHOR

Dr David Preece is head of geography for Teach First, leading on curriculum and teacher development in initial teacher education. He read geography at Oxford before studying for a PhD in climate change at University College London. He trained as a secondary teacher, taught and led departments in South East London for over a decade, completing a Masters in Education while teaching.

He is a Fellow and Chartered Geographer (Teacher) of the Royal Geographical Society, and served as a trustee of the society. He is involved with the Geographical Association, including serving on the Teacher Education Phase committee, is an En-ROADS and DfE Climate Ambassador, and is a published author and speaker in the geography, STEM, climate and education communities.

For the extras and case studies referred to throughout the book, please use the following QR code for access or see www.hachettelearning.com/john-catt/john-catt-extras.

CHAPTER 1
HOW DO WE PUT GEOGRAPHY INTO ACTION?

Since the dawn of humanity, we have been engaged in the search for three relationships. First, our relationships with one another – our tribe, our team, or our family and friends. Second, our relationship with ourselves – searching for purpose and meaning. Endless books have been written and stories told to guide these first two searches: religious interpretations, philosophies, ideologies and spiritual experiences that created and resolved conflict have risen and fallen with civilisations.

Our third relationship, too, has changed through time. It's the relationship with the world around us, the Earth in different forms. It's about how we look at, learn about, and share an understanding of the world. Like the others, this relationship has endured through time. It has provided the platform for challenges and developments, for conflicts and solutions and has revealed the worst and best of humanity. As we turn towards the next great challenge – the climate crisis – it's never been more important to be a good geographer, and to explore and understand this relationship with our Earth.

Teaching geography is a fascinating and evolving challenge and privilege. It's a great responsibility to be the guide to the world for young people, and to introduce them to some of the most complex and knotty problems of our time.

But it's not easy. With these problems come concerns, tensions and social difficulties – we have a responsibility to support our students with care and grace. The problems are nuanced, complex, and shaped often by the perspectives our students live with: their lived experience, their family life, and the cultural and conceptual understanding that they show up to our lessons carrying. And the subject itself is ever-changing – resources, case studies, technology, examples and thinking shift constantly. Even if you've planned 'the perfect lesson', it's entirely possible that it will be out of date in just a few short years. The range and breadth of our subject is enormous and that brings unique disciplinary challenges – if anything can be geography, what truly defines what it means to do geography well?

It'd be great to promise that this book holds easy answers to these questions, but it does not. Its aim is to develop and support geography

1

teachers of all backgrounds, contexts and experiences. However, my experience is in English education, and I can't claim expertise beyond that relatively narrow domain. I can't possibly do justice to all the subject specialisms, contexts and lifetime of study that geography encompasses. So, what I offer is a set of simple questions and suggestions to help you think about how you're going to put geography in action in your classroom and your context. It's a chance to explore some of the discussions and debates, and to be part of the community of geographers that are trying to help young people make sense of their place in the world. In the linked online resources, you will find case studies from geography teachers throughout England – each with their own perspective and examples that might help you. There will be lots of recommended pathways for you to explore more, and links to literature and resources that offer the chance to deepen your knowledge in the many different areas of our subject.

How do I use this book?

Of course, we too have a wide range of geographies and contexts, so some of these aspects will be more relevant to certain readers than others. We don't all teach A-level Geography, or take responsibility for designing assessments or a curriculum. Table 1 will help you identify the most relevant sections to dip in and out of.

▼ Table 1: How to use this book

If you are	You might like to start with
new to teaching geography	'Approaches to professional development' in this chapter
	How do we approach the discipline of geography?
	Whose geography do we teach?
	How do we create challenge in the classroom?
	How do we plan great geography lessons?
	How do we inspire awe and wonder in the geography classroom?
	How do we teach geographical skills in the classroom?

If you are	You might like to start with
a geography teacher looking to develop student results and outcomes	How do we sequence a geography curriculum? How do we create challenge in the geography classroom? Whose geography do we teach? How do we teach geographical skills in the classroom? How do we assess progress in the geography curriculum? How do we support students to choose geography?
a geography teacher looking to develop fieldwork and extracurricular experiences	Whose geography do we teach? How do we inspire awe and wonder in the geography classroom? How do we take geography outside the classroom? How do we plan great geography fieldwork? How do we plan for great field trips? How do we take geography beyond the curriculum?
starting to think about planning and leading a curriculum or department	How do we approach the discipline of geography? What are the debates and perspectives in the subject community? How do we sequence a geography curriculum? Whose geography do we teach? How do we create challenge in the geography classroom? How do we assess progress in the geography curriculum? How do we support students to choose geography?
starting to think about geography in the wider context and educational landscape	How do we approach the discipline of geography? What are the debates and perspectives in the subject community? Whose geography do we teach? How do we take geography beyond the curriculum? How do we support students to choose geography?

Approaches to professional development

We know that expert teaching requires mastery of the subject. It's not just what you know, it's also your ability to approach an idea from different angles, or to spot potential misconceptions in your class that make for expert teaching (EEF, 2021).

When you're planning a lesson, there's often a temptation to cover only 'the basics', or make sure you're confident about the content of that single lesson – but it doesn't take long before a well-meaning student question, or an interesting reflection and idea, can expose that preparation. Your time is precious but investing in your subject knowledge is critical. It doesn't have to be a solo exercise. Slogging away with undergraduate textbooks might work for some, but you're just as likely to develop insight and understanding by:

- Watching an expert teacher (this doesn't have to be in your own school – there are plenty of model videos online).
- Discussing content with your colleagues in school, or wherever you can. There's bound to be someone who knows and loves the topic that you're about to plan for and can give you amazing insight and resources. Don't just talk to geographers!
- Spending time with your medium-term planning and curriculum documents. This will help you understand how the lesson content and knowledge fits in to the learning journey.
- Doing what we advise GCSE and A-level students to do all the time! Don't underestimate the power of 'wider reading' and documentaries.
- Subject masterclasses, or enrichment and development courses online, can be hugely powerful and, often, they're led by experts. They obviously require investment of time and, sometimes, money but you'll have to judge the cost–benefit for yourself.

One of geography's greatest assets is the breadth and variety of our subject, but that can pose challenges when it comes to prioritising where to deepen our knowledge to develop as teachers. Sometimes, it's about developing and strengthening your geographical knowledge. This may be in terms of:

- core subject knowledge
- core subject vocabulary
- core subject diagrams

- sequencing and smallest steps
- hinterland knowledge
- wider context (**See Extras 1.1**, for access please use the QR code).

At other times, it's important to prioritise expanding your pedagogical content knowledge (PCK), which you need to best plan, sequence and explain core subject knowledge to students. There are other elements you can develop too, such as specific skills within geography, or approaches to learning and assessment. You will need to think, and judge how important each of these are to you at different moments in your career.

Developing PCK is under-rated by a lot of people but is critical if you want to be an effective teacher. You'll already know key strategies that apply to most lessons, but you there are specific ones that really come alive in geography, such as:

- case study and resource knowledge
- geography skills
- assessment for learning (formative assessment)
- summative assessment
- fieldwork and trips
- connecting to the wider geography world
- development of experience within school (**see Extras 1.2**).

The best way of improving PCK is to watch great teachers teach and talk to them about why they've made certain decisions. You should also see every single interaction, observation and conversation about your own teaching as a chance to refine and hone your skills. Be a magpie. Observe teaching in other departments: science teachers are brilliant diagram and practical explainers; RE and history teachers love enquiry just as much as we do; and English and RE teachers are amazing at dialogic teaching, discussions and debates. For something completely different, see how art, music and drama teachers are incredible at giving feedback, or look at practise and the precision of language in maths lessons. Soak it all in!

Finding professional support in the subject

You may decide that part of your professional development would be best achieved outside of your school community. In that case, you might like to look at the options offered by the Royal Geographical Society (RGS) and the Geographical Association (GA).

The Geographical Association

This is the key subject organisation for geography teachers. It:

- Supports geography teachers at primary and secondary levels, with a range of membership and volunteer options.
- Hosts an impressive set of resources on its website covering topics including teaching, curriculum and early career guidance.
- Publishes three professional journals on a termly basis: *Teaching Geography* focuses primarily on secondary and post-16 teaching.
- Commissions and publishes a wide range of reports and books including handbooks of primary and secondary geography, a number of 'toolkits' providing curriculum planning and lesson ideas, and a series of 'Top Spec' geography booklets aimed at A-level students.
- Provides a range of continuing professional development courses and events, together with quality mark schemes for primary and secondary geography.

The Royal Geographical Society

The Royal Geographical Society (with the Institute of British Geographers) (RGS-IBG) is the UK learned society for professional and academic geographers. It is a broader tent reflecting all of geography, and not exclusively focused on education. Fellows and members come from a wide range of professional backgrounds, offering lots of interesting perspectives and ideas that are potentially useful to learn from.

- The London headquarters boasts a lecture theatre, archive and one of the world's best map collections.
- The website hosts online educational resources for teachers and schools that can be sorted by theme, topic or key stage. If you're ever stuck for inspiration, they will have something that you can use!
- Their Monday-night lectures and podcasts are all excellent ways of developing your subject knowledge for free.
- If you have specific training needs, try their teacher CPD which is run by experts.

Ofsted reports on Geography

- **Subject review (Ofsted, 2021):** In 2020–21, with inspections paused under COVID-19, Ofsted took the opportunity to review the landscape for different subjects. Their aim was to synthesise research and educational thinking from several sources in order to support and inform thinking on subject education in schools. The geography review was written by former lead inspector Iain Freeland, and much of the research he drew upon was published by the subject associations and contemporary thinkers in the discipline.

- **Getting our bearings (Ofsted, 2023):** In 2022, geography teacher and author Mark Enser became the new lead inspector for geography. Through 2022 and 2023, he and his colleagues conducted a review of the subject as it was being taught and assessed in schools in England.

Both reports offer an insight into the nature and implementation of secondary geography through a particular lens. The contextual understanding of some of the wider challenges and debates in geography that they offer are helpful to teachers, but they do not give prescriptive answers to curriculum-makers as to how to solve the issues raised.

The wider geography community

There are several informal communities of practice you can become a part of. Social media offers an insight into many of the groups of the GA and RGS, and allows you to connect with many great geography educators including those involved in trust or regional leadership, or teacher education.

You may also want to look for specialist societies or, if your focus is narrow and topic-specific, free online courses from a provider such as TedX or FutureLearn. For example, the Royal Meteorological Society (RMetS) provides a course on weather (https://www.futurelearn.com/courses/come-rain-or-shine) and MetLink (https://www.metlink.org/) has a brilliant set of resources for the teaching of weather and climate. The Geological Society of London (https://www.geolsoc.org.uk/) provides expert resources on tectonics, hazards and other specialist areas. The overlap of geography and specific domains can be a helpful resource!

Equally, it's important to remember that there are a significant number of expert educators and teachers who aren't represented in any of these spaces – and their voices and reflections are just as important as those who are louder!

CHAPTER 2
HOW DO WE APPROACH THE DISCIPLINE OF GEOGRAPHY?

A geography curriculum doesn't arrive from nowhere. Geography is a hugely diverse subject, with significant overlap into other disciplinary domains and lived and learned experiences. The subject content is huge, and ever-changing, and so there needs to be a clear reason why certain things have been sampled and chosen from it. Our curriculum is fundamentally a contested concept (Gardner, 2022) as people make different decisions through time.

Change may also be driven by wider extrinsic factors – such as changes to specifications, assessment structures or the role of independent study – that affect all subjects. While these are important, having had a huge influence on the context in which we work and how we can think about our curriculum content, decisions based on them are not fundamentally geographical.

Not every subject has the same level of decision-making, agency and ownership of the curriculum as geography, and so it's worth spending some time understanding what we can do. To give the best geography to the students in front of you, I'd argue that decisions about what to teach should be grounded in the context and place that they are to be taught. But what other factors might be involved?

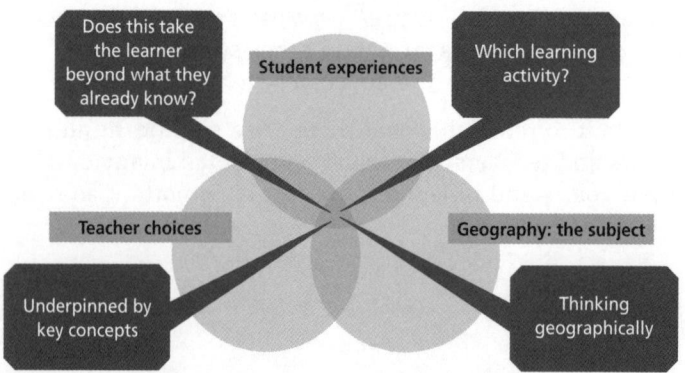

▲ Figure 1: Constructed curriculum model for geography (Gardner, 2022: 24)

A diagram from the GA (Figure 1) shows how perceptions, values and purpose can combine to shape the curriculum decisions we make as we consider lesson planning, activities and progress towards longer-term aims and goals. It reflects the different components of delivering the curriculum in your classroom (Mitchell, 2013) and suggests that there are three key challenges to teachers' decisions about what to teach:

- **What the geography really is.** The subject discipline isn't always well understood or coherently defined. An overview of the subject isn't easy for non-specialists – whether that's parents, teachers, or senior leaders – and you might have to make a case for geography as a unique discipline, rather than 'a humanity' or something interchangeable with other approaches. The subject, too, faces challenges of topics and content that are sometimes significantly contested, or moving very rapidly in terms of data, context or theories.

- **What the students bring into the lesson.** Everyone has a lived experience and, quite often, that will overlap with what they are learning or teaching. Students might have family members living in a place you're studying, or they might have parents who do the jobs that you're describing in an economic unit. This can be an incredible asset to your classroom, and add real richness and purpose to your work. It can also be challenging. There are many topics where there aren't really 'misconceptions' – just different perspectives of place, shaped by theory and lived experience. It is not always easy to reconcile what you 'should' teach with the reality of student voice, and the recognition that their perspective too, is just one experience.

- **What the teacher knows, and how they choose to enact their curriculum choices.** The subject matter of geography is constantly evolving, and there's some disparity and tension between the approach at undergraduate, graduate and school curriculum levels.

As teachers, and curriculum-makers, you are always aiming to make the best possible decisions about what to teach, and how to teach it, for your students and your context. In other subjects, these considerations may not be explored unless you are a department or trust leader. So, in the next two chapters, some of the debates and ideas about sequencing for a curriculum are explored in more detail. They include discussions about:

- How do you sequence learning for an optional subject? Do you focus on KS3, or plan for an extended learning journey through KS4 or KS5?

- How do you make choices about which components of a non-linear subject you incorporate, and in what sequence? How do your perspectives and experiences shape this?
- How do you think about the wide range of skills that are needed to function effectively as a geography student, and how do you plan to teach them?
- How do you overcome barriers and inequalities in access (for example, funding for technology, access to outdoor learning and fieldwork)?

> **Reading recommendation**
>
> Considering decision-making encompassing the entire discipline is well beyond the scope of this book but, if you're looking for a readable account of the development of secondary geography, you can read Mark Enser's work *Powerful Geography* (2021), or David Gardner's reflections in chapter 1 of *Planning Your Coherent 11–16 Curriculum* (2022), which includes some excellent analysis and critique of various geography curricula through the last five decades.
>
> You may also like to read the GA framework document (2022), which offers a conceptual overview of the discipline at high level, and how its ideas might potentially fit together.
>
> If you are interested in the history of geography as an academic discipline, Johnstone & Sidaway's *Geography and Geographers* (2016) offers an Anglo-American perspective on some of the disciplinary narratives, and the way that this is contested and constructed in the academic space. It's worth recognising that it offers a specific and narrow viewpoint that only gives context for Anglophone geography – and there's a lot more that could be explored – but it's an interesting insight into the conceptual and human-centred debates that have shaped the discipline.

What might progress in geography look like?

Whatever our conception of what geography is, and how we organise our curriculum, our intent must be that students learn and make progress. We know that our subject is not linear – so progress is rarely linear or predictable either. It's difficult to disentangle the concept of 'success at an activity or topic' with genuinely identifying progress through time, particularly when compared to more hierarchical, linear or vertical subjects like mathematics or science that have clear, sequential progression. We know, too, that we have lots of choice about how to organise the hierarchy of our curriculum.

This means that our progression model must match our curriculum model. If we've opted for concepts, we should think about what it means to develop a better conceptual understanding. If we've chosen to embed enquiry, or skills, we should be thinking about what it means to get better in those aspects, too. But can we see generalised principles of progression that are common to all geography experiences? Rawling (2007) describes three aspects of progression that are worth considering; these are shown in Table 2.

▼ Table 2: Models for progression in Geography (based on Rawling, 2007)

Progress in relation to	In practice
students' understanding and performance	Summative model of assessment: regular judgements of knowledge. Can students do more, learn more, remember more?
	Assessments may be cumulative (e.g., an end-of-year test or end-of-course exam) or the concepts may be disconnected (end-of-unit tests on different topics).
curriculum experiences planned by the teacher	Learning experiences viewed as opportunities for students to make progress.
	Progress defined as 'developing understanding through more complex activities', (i.e., the underlying assumption is that some types of assessment are intrinsically harder than others).
	Uses a combination of formative and summative techniques.
	Assessment moves from knowledge and simple recall (e.g., a 2-mark 'define this term' question), through sequences and explanations (e.g., based on diagrams, photographs) to a more complex activity or experience (e.g., a decision-making activity, an evaluative 12-mark essay question) to demonstrate a more synoptic understanding.

Progress in relation to	In practice
the inherent structure of the subject	In an ideal world, there is a sequence of content, concepts and skills that are woven together into a curriculum. This may well be true for parts of disciplines like science or mathematics. However, geography is flatter and less hierarchical: being good at one component doesn't automatically make you better at another. This makes our progression models more complex to understand.

In England, this model sits within the larger landscape of the national curriculum and the associated key stages. Figure 2 shows some statements taken from national curriculum key-stage-related expectations. For each, we're looking to see how students develop:

- contextual world knowledge of locations, places and geographical features
- understanding of conditions, processes and interactions that explain geographical features, distribution patterns and changes over space and time
- competence in geographical enquiry and the application of skills in observing, collecting, analysing, evaluating, and communicating geographical information.

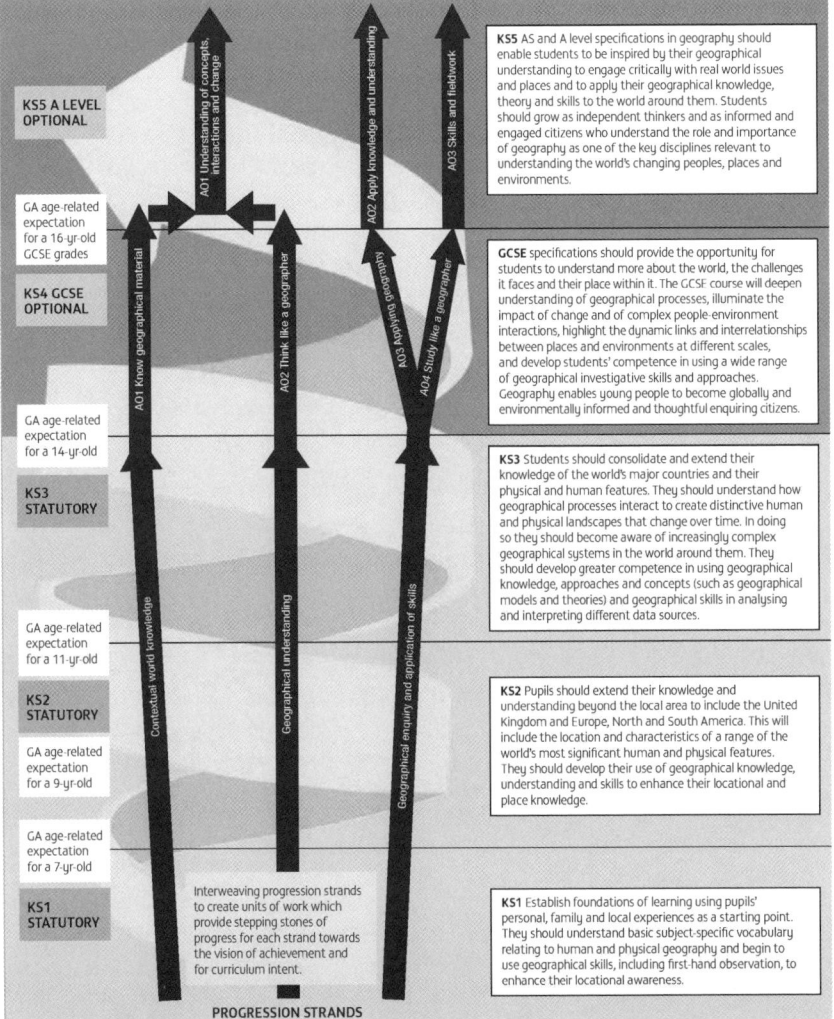

▲ Figure 2: A model of the Geography school curriculum 5–19 (Gardner, 2022: 57; adapted from Rawling, 2007: 56)

This model allows us to chart an individual course through the high-level curriculum and unpick some of the strands. The GA progression framework (Figure 3) connects national curriculum guidance to aspects of achievement and dimensions of progress, offering a vision of what it means to make progress (Gardner, 2022: 43). The aim is to support teachers planning a curriculum that is suitably ambitious, coherent and sequenced, and which delivers ambitious standards of geographical thinking over time.

Contextual world knowledge of locations, places and geographical features.

- demonstrating greater fluency with world knowledge by drawing on increasing breadth and depth of content and contexts.

Expectations by age 7	by age 9	by age 11	by age 14	by age 16
Have simple locational knowledge about individual places and environments, especially in the local area, but also in the UK and wider world.	Have begun to develop a framework of world locational knowledge, including knowledge of places in the local area, UK and wider world, and some globally significant physical and human features.	Have a more detailed and extensive framework of knowledge of the world, including globally significant physical and human features and places in the news.	Have extensive knowledge relating to a wide range of places, environments and features at a variety of appropriate spatial scales, extending from local to global.	Have a broader and deeper understanding of locational contexts, including greater awareness of the importance of scale and the concept of global.

Understanding of the conditions, processes and interactions that explain features, distribution patterns, and changes over time and space.

- extending from the familiar and concrete to the unfamiliar and abstract
- making greater sense of the world by organising and connecting information and ideas about people, places, processes and environments
- working with more complex information about the world, including the relevance of people's attitudes, values and beliefs.

Expectations by age 7	by age 9	by age 11	by age 14	by age 16
Show understanding by describing the places and features they study using simple geographical vocabulary, identifying some similarities and differences and simple patterns in the environment.	Demonstrate their knowledge and understanding of the wider world by investigating places beyond their immediate surroundings, including human and physical features and patterns, how places change and some links between people and environments. They become more adept at comparing places, and understand some reasons for similarities and differences.	Understand in some detail what a number of places are like, how and why they are similar and different, and how and why they are changing. They know about some spatial patterns in physical and human geography, the conditions that influence those patterns, and the processes that lead to change. They show some understanding of the links between places, people and environments.	Understand the physical and human conditions and processes that lead to the development of, and change in, a variety of geographical features, systems and places. They can explain various ways in which places are linked and the impact such links have on people and environments. They can make connections between different geographical phenomena they have studied.	Gain a deeper understanding of the processes that lead to geographical changes and the multivariate nature of human-physical relationships and interactions, with a stronger focus on forming valid generalisations and abstractions, together with a growing awareness of the importance of theoretical perspectives and conceptual frameworks in geography.

Competence in **geographical enquiry**, and the application of skills in observing, collecting, analysing, evaluating and communicating geographical information.

- increasing the range and accuracy of pupils' investigative skills, and advancing their ability to select and apply these with increasing independence to geographical enquiry.

Expectations by age 7	by age 9	by age 11	by age 14	by age 16
Be able to investigate places and environments by asking and answering questions, making observations and using sources such as simple maps, atlases, globes, images and aerial photos.	Be able to investigate places and environments by asking and responding to geographical questions, making observations and using sources such as maps, atlases, globes, images and aerial photos. They can express their opinions and recognise that others may think differently.	Be able to carry out investigations using a range of geographical questions, skills and sources of information including a variety of maps, graphs and images. They can express and explain their opinions, and recognise why others may have different points of view.	Be able, with increasing independence, to choose and use a wide range of data to help investigate, interpret, make judgements and draw conclusions about geographical questions, issues and problems, and express and engage with different points of view about these.	Be able to plan and undertake independent enquiry in which skills, knowledge and understanding are applied to investigate geographical questions, and show competence in a range of intellectual and communication skills, including the formulation of arguments, that include elements of synthesis and evaluation of material.

▲ Figure 3: The GA progression framework (Gardner, 2022: 44)

Following the national curriculum means that aspects of this curriculum progression are outlined for us as expectations. In Table 3, you can see how students should make progress between Year 7 and Year 9, based on different themes. This gives a broad approach to structuring progress in KS3 in accordance with the main objectives. These should then link to the assessment objectives for higher key stages, which have been laid out in the specifications from awarding bodies (Table 4). Notice that these progression frameworks do not specify concepts, topics or content to be studied.

▼ Table 3: Aspects of progression in geography (Gardner, 2022)

Aspect of geography	Year 7	Year 9	Comment
Vocabulary	Using a limited vocabulary	Precise use of a wider range of Tier 2 vocabulary	Students develop accurate and precise use of geographical vocabulary
Knowledge of place	Geographical knowledge of some places	Understanding of a wider range of places and links between them	Students broaden their scale and contexts of study and explain the links between places
Human & physical patterns and process	Describing patterns and processes	Explaining patterns and processes	Students begin to cope with increasingly complex patterns and processes
Geographical thinking	Participating in practical activities involving geographical thinking, or close proxies	Building increasingly abstract models of real situations	Students understand increasingly complex abstract ideas, and are capable of operating within abstract ideas
Geographical explanation	Explaining events and geographical phenomena in terms of their own ideas	Explaining these in terms of accepting ideas, models, or using generalisations	Explanations become more accurate and precise; students increasingly recognise links, interrelationships and complexity

Aspect of geography	Year 7	Year 9	Comment
Geographical enquiry	Following teacher guidance for investigations	Forming relevant geographical questions and investigating them systematically	Students increasingly understand the meaning of geographical enquiry and the steps they need to carry it out and present findings
Map skills	Using simple drawings and maps	Using a wide range of maps and diagrams, and selecting the most appropriate way to use them to represent information	Students make increasing use of cognitive skills for interpretation, analysis and communication
Fieldwork	Guided practical activities	Working independently outside the classroom	Students, with increasing independence, use geographical skills in more complex and precise ways

▼ Table 4: Progression in aims and assessment objectives for 11–19 (adapted from Gardner, 2018; 2022)

National curriculum KS3	Contextual world knowledge of locations, places and geographical features	Understanding conditions, processes and interactions that explain geographical features, distribution patterns and changes over space and time	Competence in geographical enquiry and the application of skills in observing, collecting, analysing, evaluating, and communicating geographical information
GCSE aims	Know geographical material	Think like a geographer	Study like a geographer — Applying geography
GCSE assessment objectives	AO1: 15% Demonstrate knowledge of locations, places, processes, environments and different scales	AO2: 25% Demonstrate geographical understanding of concepts and how they are used in relation to places, environments and processes, and the interrelationships between places, environments and processes	AO3: 35% Apply knowledge and understanding to interpret, analyse and evaluate geographical information and issues AO4: 25% Select, adapt and use a variety of skills and techniques to investigate questions and issues and make judgements, and communicate findings
A-Level assessment objectives	AO1: 30–40% Demonstrate knowledge and understanding of places, environments, concepts, processes, interactions and change at a variety of scales		AO2: 30–40% Apply knowledge and understanding in different contexts to interpret, analyse and evaluate geographical information and issues AO3: 20–30% Use a variety of relevant quantitative, qualitative and fieldwork skills to: Investigate geographical questions and issues Interpret, analyse and evaluate data and evidence Construct arguments and draw conclusions

There are a lot of complicated factors behind curricular decision-making in geography, and these change through time. The expertise and experience of our team alters as colleagues take on new roles, or move to different schools. With global events moving at a rapid pace, particular topics may become more or less relevant, and a curriculum unit which was topical and loved by students when you first taught it might now seem outdated and irrelevant. Our schools and communities may shift over time, and the lived experience of our students gently ebbs and flows with that tide. And so it's critical to remember that there are no 'correct' solutions to these challenges – there are only those which serve a context and community at a particular point in time. Curriculum is a conversation (Myatt, 2018) and, in geography perhaps more than most subjects, it's quite a fast-paced chat. Recognising this – and acknowledging that you, as a geography teacher, will be doing curriculum work in a different way to some of your colleagues – is a key first step in understanding and being able to own this conversation for your context and community (Mitchell, 2013).

Thankfully, there are some ways to approach this conversation that help you to make sense of the landscape. Some of them are philosophies of curriculum design, while others offer ways of working within a curriculum for Mode A and Mode B thinking (Sherrington, 2017). Some options can work together really well: you may have a 'powerful geography' curriculum with enquiry focused on the decision-making end of a unit or approached through embedded fieldwork. You may choose to scale your curriculum around key concepts and embed enquiry questions in multiple layers.

Let's look at some approaches that may help to cohere curriculum thinking.

Approaches to geography: conceptual frameworks

Geographical concepts are the high-level ideas that represent the bigger picture of the subject. They aim to overlap with lots of the content of the discipline – 'what geographers know and how they think'. They are ideas to be explored and used in themselves, but also can be ways of organising materials, which is how they are often used in curriculum-making by teachers.

Many curricula, including the national curriculum of England and Wales between 1991 and 2000, identify three major themes: space, place and environment (see for example, GA & RGS 2011; Lambert & Jones, 2013; Rawling, 2016; GA, 2022). However, others use themes such as Earth systems and processes, or 'scale, place, space and time' showing that even at the top level there is not universal agreement (Lambert & Morgan, 2010; Lambert & Jones, 2013; DfE 2013).

The GA curriculum framework (GA 2022: 7) also identifies *organising concepts*, which they define as the 'perspectives that are needed to consider substantive content, and to provide a common language within which to consider the different operational dimensions of geographical thought.' These – like 'second-order concepts' in history – help geography teachers to shape and sequence the geography content in a way that illustrates disciplinary knowledge over time (Rawling, 2008). The curriculum framework uses five of these – time, scale, diversity, interconnection and interpretation. Together, these combine to give a conceptual grid that can illustrate diverse ways of organising thinking and processes in your geography curriculum. Of these, it's arguably interconnection (or synopticity) that gives geography the strongest disciplinary identity. Maude (2016) argues that interconnection is the 'basis for geography's claim to be an integrative discipline' – and it's common for us to explain the 'geographical lens' and the relationship between ideas as the key feature that makes geography distinctive.

For example, Table 5 shows ways of looking at the relationship between these organising concepts and major concepts. This isn't indicative of case studies, examples or places you might study, but some of the themes of topics or curriculum thinking.

▼ Table 5: A conceptual grid for school geography (after GA, 2022)

	Time	Scale	Diversity	Interconnection	Interpretation
	Continuity versus change	Local, regional or micro, macro	Similarity and difference	Independent, contingent, hierarchy or decisions	Perspectives or representations
Place	How do places change over time? Why do places change over time? How do people feel about places, or how does place shape people's identity?	What is our local place? What is our regional place? What is our national place? How does globalisation change our sense of place?	What does our local place have as key features? How does our place compare to another place? How does our culture compare to a different culture? How do people belong to places?	How are our places connected? How are places linked and organised?	How do I feel about place? How do we tell stories about places, and how do we construct our sense of place? How do people's sense of place differ? How do we represent different places?
Space	How do our distributions, networks and locations change over time?	How do we connect local to global scales? How does transport change our scale?	How are our places and spaces the same or different to others? How do we compare our spaces?	What are the patterns we see through space? How are we connecting and relating them?	How do different people describe networks and spatial connections? What role does geopolitics play?

	Time	Scale	Diversity	Interconnection	Interpretation
Earth systems	What are the timescales that the Earth's processes operate on? What do we know about stable or dynamic systems? What do we mean by equilibrium, change or tipping points?	What are the physical scales of the Earth's processes? Is there an Anthropocene, and what does it mean?	How do Earth's systems, adaptations and modifications show similarity and difference? What difference has climate change made to our Earth systems?	How are the Earth's systems connected and interdependent? What are the roles of feedback processes and natural cycles?	How do people have different perspectives on the Earth's systems or processes? Why and how do they construct those views? How do we fairly represent them?
Environment	How and where are climate change impacts accelerating or changing?	How have the human impacts changed the natural world at different scales?	How have environments been modified by human actions? What are the shared and varied responses to environmental responsibility?	How does our dependence on the planet shape our response to climate change? How do we feel responsible for the planet?	Why do people have different approaches to managing the environment? How do we fairly represent those approaches?

The GA curriculum framework (2022) suggests some key questions to use when developing your curriculum:

- What are the key areas of knowledge and understanding that you think geography includes and, therefore, what key concepts do you need to include?
- What further significant organising ideas are fundamental to understanding?
- How do more specific, concrete examples and knowledge of locations relate to these key concepts?
- How do our key concepts and conceptual frameworks help us make sense of the world and allow geographers to generate new knowledge?

Critical reflection

It's hard to imagine that there's geography curriculum content which doesn't have *some* conceptual structures embedded within it. Most commonly, you'll see scale – from local to global – used to arrange or develop progression. You may see some distinct language and frameworks which reference the national curriculum approaches or language, and lean on its ideas. Often, the organising concepts are embedded through the structure of a unit of work – going from concrete to more abstract notions of interpretation or diversity as themes.

But, as we'll see in a later chapter, these are often more subtly structured than some other approaches to curriculum – they are woven in through the content and disciplinary thinking. This might be challenging to unpick – particularly if you are supporting non-specialist teachers – whereas other curriculum themes and approaches might be more obvious!

Approaches to geography: Geographical enquiry

Geographical enquiry is a student-centred approach to learning that involves students constructing geographical knowledge by making sense of new information (Roberts, 2023). Unlike an open-ended 'inquiry learning' model where everyone is working on different things, and heading in different directions, enquiry learning is often fairly cohesive and controlled by the teacher. This is important for the discipline of geography (Roberts, 2023), because:

- It acknowledges that geographical knowledge is not 'out there' as some absolute reality but that it has been constructed by geographers. When students are learning geography through enquiry, they are learning about the nature of geographical knowledge, and how it is the type of questions that are asked that is important. It models 'geographical thinking' and disciplinary knowledge as a process.

- It involves students in making sense of new information for themselves. When they learn something new, they have to engage with it to incorporate it into what they already know; an enquiry approach can help them do this.
- Learning geography through enquiry can develop 'geographical skills'. It includes using information presented in different forms, media and digital literacies, problem solving, collaborating, and communicating. It can also help students to see, understand and appreciate the world differently by encouraging them to think critically about geographical information.
- Geography enquiries are required by public examinations, latterly as the Non-Examined Assessment at A-level. There is also a mandated requirement to conduct fieldwork at Key Stage 4.

In this disciplinary-inspired approach to learning, students extend their geographical knowledge and learn skills at the same time. There are four key characteristics to an enquiry approach:

- It is question driven. Curiosity and questioning run through a unit of work.
- Is supported by evidence from the real world, not imagined examples. Students need to collect, interpret and analyse a range of geographical sources to make sense of the information and evidence.
- It requires 'thinking geographically', by reasoning, weighing evidence and considering different viewpoints. It requires development of knowledge and conceptual understanding.
- It is reflective. Students reach conclusions, make judgements, and develop their own viewpoints. Enquiry encourages students to think critically about what they have learned.

To teach geography through enquiry, Roberts argues that it is important to establish a culture of enquiry in the classroom through the fabric of a curriculum. This means that students are encouraged to question, to examine geographical sources critically and to think geographically for themselves. An investigative approach needs to permeate everything you do, from introducing and debriefing activities, though discussions to how you respond to what students write.

Critical reflection

Geographical enquiry has the strongest connection to the discipline of geography, and is the approach that has been established longest in the classroom and culture of teaching and learning. Undergraduate geographers will likely remember their own dissertations as the highlight of their curriculum journey!

Enquiry approaches might often be used to construct a unit or frame a particular topic, or part of a topic. You'll see enquiry-style approaches in decision-making exercises, for example. Some curriculum-makers will have enquiry as the framing 'big questions' that shape a scheme of work.

For geographical enquiry to work at its best, it's important to acknowledge Roberts' bigger ideas. It requires a culture of curiosity and learning about the world, and deliberately embedding, practising and giving time in lessons to the skills of geography: handling sources, data, making judgements and connections. Giving an 'enquiry title' to a unit where students do no thinking, and have little scope to explore data or produce alternative answers does not do justice to the concept.

This may suit some school approaches more than others, and teachers will need to understand how to best apply that to their own context. There are always opportunities to do enquiries within your lessons – creating a need to know, exploring and hypothesising about data and outcomes, and coming to reasoned conclusions. This is the heart of what it means to do geography well.

Approaches to geography: Powerful geography

'Powerful knowledge' has been widely referred to in different spheres and the idea can be often misused and misapplied. In geography, 'powerful knowledge' or 'powerful disciplinary knowledge' (Enser, 2021) has a history and particular purpose.

The concept was introduced by Michael Young in 2008. His argument was that the school curriculum was constructed by, and for, the ruling elites – and was intended to impart the knowledge of the powerful. Geography, with embedded connections to empire and environmental determinism, was a key part of this – and this legacy is still one of the biggest issues for us to tackle, as a later chapter will explore. Young argued that the post-modern reaction was to create a generic skills-based curriculum, based around student interests and experiences. This led to placing 'the geography of' in front of almost any word to form a unit of teaching. You may have experienced this yourself and been taught 'the geography of sport', or 'the geography of crime'.

This emphasis on generic skills does not enable young people to gain an understanding beyond their own experience. Teachers should be giving students ideas and experiences that move them beyond what they have already experienced, and providing specialised knowledge to give them the ability to think about and do things that they couldn't before. Young called this 'powerful' not because it had power over students, but because it gave them power (Gardner, 2022: 26).

Alaric Maude (2016: 75) – an Australian geographer – wanted to be able to identify what made knowledge powerful. He suggested it was knowledge that:

- provides students with 'new ways of thinking about the world'
- provides students with new ways of analysing, explaining and understanding the world
- gives students power over their own knowledge
- enables young people to follow and participate in debates on significant local, national and global issues
- is knowledge of the world.

Young & Muller (2010) have sketched out the different outcomes of knowledge thinking in describing three future scenarios – broadly aligned to the themes of traditional/knowledge-led, progressive/skills-led, or progressive/knowledge-led.

The latter 'Future 3' model has been picked up by a number of projects, including the GeoCapabilities project (Mitchell, 2022; Walshe & Perry, 2022). In his book on powerful geography, Mark Enser (2021) writes about it more extensively and offers practical advice on how to structure and conceptualise a Future 3 curriculum in geography.

The powerful geography model places significant emphasis on the teacher as curriculum-maker – they have a decisive role in making the right decision about what to study to give the most powerful opportunity for their students to progress. This approach is echoed by contemporary trends in secondary geography (Hesslewood, 2023), where it is the decisions and intent of the schools and teachers that is most important.

> A successful geography curriculum reflects teachers' careful thought about what is to be taught, the rationale for it, the sequencing of learning and the relationships between the forms of knowledge. With this in place, students are likely to know, remember and be able to do more.
>
> (Ofsted, 2021)

Critical reflection

Powerful knowledge has become associated with a particular time and sequence of education thinking in the English school system, and there are undoubtedly ideological and educational debates around that relationship. But I think at the heart of the principles is a positive and place-based question: what are the most important things that our students need to know? What choices do we make to support that?

This – as I've said before – might be different for different contexts. An urban school near a river might make a different decision about what topics their students need to explore than a rural school on the coast. The role of specific curriculum-makers and teacher agency can often be overlooked in assumptions about what is the 'most powerful' knowledge – it is always contextual! Done well, and thoughtfully curated, a powerful geography curriculum has immense strength. Poorly implemented – perhaps heavily inspired by a location and context that does not transfer to your own – it will not serve your students well.

Although there is often an ideological or experiential crossover between powerful geography and other forms of educational paradigm (such as direct instruction, or Mode A teaching), it's important to recognise that powerful geography rarely prescribes a method of teaching. It asks you, as curriculum-maker, to focus on the knowledge and outcomes you want, not how you get there. It's perfectly plausible, therefore, to have a powerful curriculum that combines with geographical enquiry and meaningful geographical skill development!

These approaches give us a sequence of what progress in geographical learning might look like, while still enabling curriculum-makers to choose what, where and how students learn the geographical content.

But this means there's still a range of ideas and concepts, so there are debates and discussions in the geography community about the best ways to teach, the best options to choose, and how to make decisions about sequencing. These will be the focus of the next two chapters.

CHAPTER 3
WHAT ARE THE DEBATES AND PERSPECTIVES IN THE SUBJECT COMMUNITY?

The nature of geography as an academic discipline is to explore contextual understanding and show curiosity about different perspectives, and so too is the nature of many geography teachers and students. There's an intrinsic acceptance that there are lots of perspectives, and there's room for many inside what is quite a big, loose academic tent. The subject community tends to have a range of views, values and ideas, and consider different parts of the discipline important (Bustin, 2018).

Some of these conversations have been going on for some time (see, e.g., Lambert & Jones, 2013; Maude, 2016): they are challenges that remain at the heart of what it is to do geography in a changing world, and under increasing financial and delivery pressure in secondary schools (Rawlings Smith & Kinder, 2023). Other parts of the modern dialogue have emerged as themes in more recent years; and no doubt will be replaced by further iterations, and new ideas, in times to come.

How much geography are we teaching?

There's a lot of content that could be covered in geography lessons and, if we want to realistically prepare students to engage with the wider world as thoughtful citizens, there's an ever-changing palette of news, current events and critical thinking that could be added on top.

The current national curriculum for geography and exam specifications have been stable for nearly a decade. But, while teachers and curriculum-makers have been able to make their way through on their chosen paths, there is often little coherence between the ways that people choose to deliver it. We cannot reasonably say that there is 'a' geography curriculum in the current system: optionality and curriculum decisions mean that few students will experience an identical curriculum.

There is far more agreement that there is a lot of content to cover, and that the content makes high demands of vocabulary and literacy at KS4. Few teachers have time at GCSE to explore wider contexts and settings, and recent reports have identified a significant challenge whereby the specification effectively becomes the curriculum (Ofsted, 2023). The current prescribed content adds significant pressure on schools to 'deliver' rather than 'explore'.

Whose geographies are we teaching?

The pressure to cover content has often led to pressure on resources, examples and case studies. Over time, this has drifted in to more challenging issues of poor representation, over-simplification, and geography content that no longer reflects the modern world. In a multicultural and diverse Britain, being ignorant or misrepresenting the experience of our past and present, and our students' lives, is a significant disservice to them – and to geography.

One of the biggest areas of collective subject effort over the past five years has been around representation of multiple geographies. We need to think carefully about how we choose to represent the world. Whose voices, examples and case studies do we use? How do we show complexity and diversity in all forms? What choices do we make? What do we hide? But we also need to acknowledge the legacies of power, colonialism and inequity that sit at the heart of our discipline, and grapple with the way they influence our subject and how we teach it. It's a huge debate, which sits in chapter 5.

What geographers are we creating? How representative are we?

Although more popular as an options choice than it has been in many years (Brace & Souch, 2020) the analysis of who studies geography at GCSE, A-level and university reveal trends in socio-economic status and ethnicity that are not reflective of wider society.

Several reports and analyses have shown that geography remains predominantly a white, middle-class subject, particularly at university level (Brace & Souch, 2020; Dorling, 2019). This, of course, has direct implications for the representation of geographers in the wider professional sphere but, critically, it shapes who is eligible to be a geography teacher and continues the cycle. A 2021 report by the RGS showed the impacts of this on student participation in geography and related options and careers.

There is clearly more work to be done in this space, and there are plenty of perspectives and debates on the goals and best ways to achieve them (GA, 2025). The intersection of representation, ethnicity, socio-economic status and what it means to be inclusive is an extensive challenge that our subject faces, and we'll explore that further in a later chapter. It's important to reflect on how your geography community reflects your wider context and community.

How is our fieldwork provision? What challenges does it face?

There is little debate about the role and importance of fieldwork in geography: the need for it is part of our disciplinary tradition and it is a mandatory requirement for GCSE and A-level students, (although optional and more varied at KS3).

So where are the issues? Unfortunately, we know that despite near-universal agreement on the purpose and importance of fieldwork, it is often not consistently delivered as an experience, or as a curriculum process in schools (Ofsted, 2023). There are two separate strands to disentangle here.

In a landscape of educational-funding austerity and a wider cost-of-living challenge, it is no surprise that fieldwork budgets and delivery have been squeezed. Schools report transport or coach costs doubling or tripling, accommodation and expert provider support becoming increasingly expensive, and families less able to support additional expenses. The Covid-19 pandemic has had a compounding effect: the lessening of experience or requirement during the initial lockdown phases led to a lingering resistance to put it back into an already challenging timetable. Although subject associations, providers and related organisations are keen to promote and support fieldwork, there is still substantial discussion about how best to ensure that provision is equitably accessed by all schools and all students.

The longer-term academic debate centres around the quality of fieldwork, and what it means to make progress or develop in it through time. There is little agreement on what fieldwork progression or curriculum thinking in this area might look like, and even less coherence on how to implement that across multiple key stages or different schools. This leads to confusion and tensions – particularly in schools where there is blurring between fieldwork as a disciplinary exercise and field trips as positive

29

cultural capital experiences. This is not a new debate – discussions on this topic have occupied the landscape for several decades now. In 2025, the Geographical Association published a report on high-quality geography fieldwork for all (Kitchen, 2025), offering a sense of progression models and potential frameworks for the evaluation of fieldwork, which may be a significant and useful first step towards coherence. We'll explore this further in chapter 11.

How are we making space to teach geographical skills? What are we teaching?

We know that 'being a geographer' involves a synoptic blend of analysis, numerical and graphical competence, and spatial and mapping literacy, which needs fluent communication skills to explain well. Roberts' work on enquiry (2023) focuses just as much on the tools of enquiry as on what is being looked at. 'Knowledge rich' pedagogies can be delivered at the expense of a deliberate and thoughtful integration of essential skills.

Lesson patterns, combined with the variations in our content and approach, mean that even those with the best curriculum intent will find it challenging to ensure that all skills are covered frequently enough to build procedural fluency.

Unlike fieldwork, it's also important to be mindful of the potential for cross-curricular discussion and development or tension in this space. We can expect the skills of numeracy and graphicacy to be encountered and taught in other subjects and, although this may appear to be an effective solution, it rarely works like that in practice. The discussion around how to teach skills is continued in chapter 9.

How are we including geospatial technologies and GIS in our curriculum?

While many skills overlap with other subjects, the emergence of geospatial technologies and geographic information systems (GIS) is a uniquely subject-specific problem that has been discussed repeatedly in recent years. As with fieldwork and wider skills, there is little agreement on what 'good' or 'progression' might look like; and experiences with a GIS platform are often dotted into individual lessons, rather than a coherent curriculum. There is no real driving force behind this: while GIS and use of technology are recommended, they are not essential parts of a specification for compliance, nor are there any assessments at this stage which rely on students having confidence with GIS.

It's likely that schools have even greater inequity in terms of their GIS provision than of fieldwork experience. Schools facing budget cuts and curriculum pressure simply do not have resources to put many computers in geography classrooms, and a digital divide stretches the gap further. It takes a significant amount of time, teacher knowledge and expert instruction to build up the procedural and platform expertise to access high-quality geographical thinking, and these issues combine to generate a wide range of school experiences of GIS (Ofsted, 2023).

Non-specialist teachers in geography

Despite geography being more popular than ever as a GCSE and A-level option, the pipeline of qualified teachers to create, curate and engage in a high-quality curriculum is shrinking (Preece & Tapsfield, 2023). In part, we are a victim of our own success: having marketed geography as a way to get high-quality, green and purposeful jobs, we cannot be particularly surprised when students go on to choose such positive and rewarding careers. In other respects, geography is no different to teaching as a wider profession (McLean et al., 2024), which has faced significant recruitment challenges in a hybrid, flexible and cost-conscious world.

It is no longer guaranteed that schools have a specialist geography teacher at KS3. Most schools will, understandably, prioritise their KS4 and KS5 classes and, increasingly, we are seeing a significant portion of KS3 lessons taught by non-specialist teachers (Ofsted, 2023; Preece & Tapsfield, 2023). While there is undoubted good will and positive engagement from these teachers, it is not reasonable to expect them to be able to replicate the disciplinary knowledge, skills and experiences that a specialist teacher would have developed through their subject training and career (Rawlings Smith & Kinder, 2023).

There is considerable debate about the best solutions for this challenge. Some schools have adopted centralised curriculum provision and models. This might be through a trust leader for geography, with shared resources and booklets, or an external provider of resources (e.g., Ark's Mastery Curriculum, Oak National resources, the GA KS3 *Teachers' Toolkit*, or their *Geography 11–14* series of textbooks). Inevitably, these compromise the bespoke curriculum creation of a local school context, replacing it with standardised, coherent resources. Alternatively, departments may choose to actively engage and support non-specialists in the teaching of their own curriculum, with implications for workload and, potentially, teacher wellbeing.

As with so many other issues, there is intersectional inequity in the experience of this. Some schools find it harder to recruit than others – due to location, reputation (including outcomes or current Ofsted rating), potential salary scales, or social, economic or community contexts. There is widespread, and often intense, debate on solutions for this school experience, and for the wider teacher education and recruitment issues. Idea and value overlaps often further complicate the discussions.

How is our subject facing the climate crisis?

The debate should no longer be 'if' we are facing a climate crisis, but how best to mitigate and adapt to the changes we see in the news and the world around us. Within the geography community, there are some challenges that this poses for us.

First, how do we teach and empower our students to engage and explore this issue with hope (Alcock, 2024) rather than anxiety (Rackley, 2020)? This is a contentious issue, and subject knowledge and curriculum planning is vital. A significant number of competing 'climate education' programmes now exist, and the choice and options that teachers and curriculum-makers face is potentially overwhelming. There is a significant risk that resources will be adopted 'off the shelf' and inherit approaches and resources for climate change education that are not geographical in their nature. Ecosystems, meteorological or engineering approaches may all add value and richness to our discussions – but it is how they are brought together coherently and synoptically that is at the heart of geography education. You need to carefully consider what resources and approaches to climate education are being explored in your local context, and why.

Second, what is the role and identity of geography as a subject? It has been suggested that the climate concerns of young people are one of the key drivers behind recent increases in uptake of geography GCSE and A-level across the country. There are potential risks to the reputation of our discipline if the wider perception is that 'all we do is climate change'. It is vital to preserve the broad and rich heritage of our academic tradition (Livingstone, 1992): as important as climate change is to teach, it cannot be all that we do.

At the same time, it's important to be mindful of the risks. The Department for Education's *Sustainability and Climate Change Strategy* (DfE, 2022) brought forward several initiatives, including a natural history GCSE option, carbon literacy training, and the development of national education nature parks and climate leaders' awards. Explicit reference was made to the national climate education action plan in setting up an independent expert body (including members such as the RMetS, STEM Learning, Association of Science Teaching) for 'the validation and creation of climate education resources that support the delivery of the national curriculum', but without recognition or membership from geography associations, educators and voices.

This tension is critical for an options subject to grasp and understand. We need to remain relevant and engaging, so young people choose geography, but without losing sight of our disciplinary heritage and core concepts. There are several different perspectives on this, and conversations will continue to try to persuade and influence at strategic level, but it is important to acknowledge this debate as part of the discussions around curriculum-making and its influence on options choices in your own context.

The range of debates, perspectives and conceptualisations of geography can feel overwhelming to begin with. It's fair to say that there is not universal agreement on what geography is for, let alone what the best way to teach it at secondary level is. But I think that's probably one of the greatest strengths of our discipline. We are diverse and pluralist in our approach. We offer a range of ways that you can do the subject: you can be flexible to match purpose, values and context. In part, that reflects some of the human context of our subject. We all bring different humanity and lived experience to our thinking and our way of seeing the world. We all want to explore and identify the things we choose to value or explore. I think, in part, it's a conscious decision – as we've seen in the past in our academic history (Johnston & Sidaway, 2016) – to reject the utilitarian mindset that has seen geography's traditions used for immoral and unjust purposes. We can and must do better than we have before.

CHAPTER 4
HOW DO WE SEQUENCE A GEOGRAPHY CURRICULUM?

We've already outlined a sense of the complexity and challenges of a geography curriculum in the modern landscape. There are a lot of topics, concepts and structures that you may follow or consider, and there are few structures that are universally accepted as 'the geography curriculum' – even with a national curriculum and exam specifications as guidelines.

> Leaders appreciate the structure of the subject, so their curriculum plans are constructed effectively to ensure that students know more, remember more and are able to do more.
>
> **(Ofsted, 2021)**

The elegant simplicity of this statement masks a range of challenges. We intend students to learn and make progress through time. We want to be able to use formative and summative assessment to support and direct our teaching towards that intent. However, progression in geography is rarely linear. Geographical knowledge develops partially by ideas becoming more abstract or more difficult, or by accumulating more synoptic content about the world (Gardner, 2022). But it's hard to make practical judgements about what that means for individual topics and ideas. Are rivers harder than coasts? Are glaciers easier than those? What makes an A-level study of settlement different to a GCSE study, or a Year 7 one? Do they know more places? Remember more terminology? Or is it more complex? How do skills fit within this?

Over time, these ideas of 'progression' have become more difficult, and there is still significant disagreement in the profession as to what it means to get 'better at geography'. We occupy a contested discipline, and so it's important to make the connection between what we're teaching and how we design and think about our assessment of it, and for this to be adapted and tailored to our context.

> **Reading recommendation**
>
> David Gardner's *Planning your coherent 11–16 geography curriculum* (2022) covers the principles and history behind a number of key ideas and offers a practical and thoughtful approach to implementing some curriculum design ideas. Gardner's experience in exam boards, the QCA and leadership of assessment thinking is really helpful in unpicking the nature of progress, and how to plan for it well.

High-level considerations for curriculum-makers

So, what are the key questions to consider when you're choosing your topics and creating your big curriculum building blocks? There are often big structural and pragmatic considerations to dovetail with the geographical ones. Some of these may be derived as an individual, or as a department, but I think most of them come from wider contexts and a school or trust landscape.

How big is your horizon?

What is the context and landscape you are working within? Do you teach in an all-through, 11–16 or 11–18 school? Are you planning a three-year KS3, or two years? Do you want to connect it to a five-year KS3–4, or a seven-year KS3–5? Is there a minimum entitlement that you want all your students to experience, whether they continue with geography as an options choice or not? How do you balance the breadth and depth options?

Begin with the end: What is your vision for geography?

You may have a vision that has been constructed as a department and a team, or a specific intent to tailor towards a whole-school vision for what you want your students to achieve at the end of their schooling. You may have specific experiences in mind (travel, topics, knowledge), or specific outcomes in terms of citizenship, enquiry or skill development.

Depth, or breadth?

The notion of a spiral curriculum is popular, and the idea of revisiting topics with increasingly complex or larger-scale perspectives can have a conceptual appeal for some geography leads. For others, there are far too many potential topics to cover to do some twice (or three times). Whatever your philosophical stance, the implementation is also important. There are too many students who only ever study rivers and coasts at KS3, and then again at GCSE, and again at A-level – but struggle to develop the depth, complexity or synopticity that a truly effective spiral curriculum would deliver. There may be students who are excited by breadth and studying new topics at GCSE or reassured by the familiarity of topics they've seen before. Your context and knowledge of your students is important, and you need to acknowledge the pragmatic implications of this decision-making!

What are your core themes and scales?

There are many different approaches to an academic geography curriculum, and it's important for you to identify what yours are. You might want to embed enquiry throughout. You may have a focus on fieldwork and ensuring all year groups get out to do geography. You may have a conceptual focus on place or space, or you may want to focus on a scalar story – going from local, to regional to global. This gives you a sense of a broad structure of your curriculum journey, and helps you to identify what topics, themes or areas of study might fit that sequence best.

How do you want to incorporate skills?

Alongside the geographical content, there are a lot of ideas that need to be subtly explored to 'do geography' effectively. In an ideal world, it's helpful to know what you want to achieve in this regard as you design a curriculum, and to be able to think about how you might build and incorporate cross-curricular elements where appropriate. You may need to know a bit more about your school's curriculum and intent, or even some of the resources and features that are available to you.

What are the features of your terrain?

Several geographical considerations may be partnered with thinking about the infrastructure and landscape of your timetable and teaching. If you have regular and consistent access to computer facilities, you might plan a different approach to geographical enquiry than if you have none. Your timetable may guide the number of lessons, blocking, or some features of how you can teach. This, in turn, might support different topics, choices, or the options available with a term or half term. You may have to consider common lesson resources, or the use of booklets instead of textbooks, or even the extent to which you have staff confident in physical or human topics.

What are the key drivers from your own context?

All of our schools are potentially different, with key features of place (location, size of school, gender balance, community and demographic context) shaping educational features like intake size, the typical number of GCSE options groups, or perhaps even the scope of the school and whether you have a sixth form. Schools will have significant variance in funding, and the extent to which subjects and department budgets are prioritised – you may have lots of resources and money to spend, or you may have very little. Within that framework, you and your school will have some key priorities for your students. It may be that you want your under-served rural community to experience the contrast of a big-city experience. You might want to deliberately utilise the wide range of your community's experience to give meaningful engagement with a representative view of the world and the lived experience of your families. You might have a deliberate intent to take your students from an inner-city London school to the coast, or to an upland former glacial area. These are hugely individual and valuable decisions, and they need to be sympathetically and carefully considered in a specific context.

What might this look like in practice?

Curriculum design is – and should be – an ongoing conversation with the context, community and intended outcomes, and it can change with evaluation, academic success or the evolution of a school, department and staff. Schools and geography departments are living and breathing ecosystems, and a change of leadership, staff turnover or a wider shift might have far more impact on our curriculum plans than we imagine!

So, there's no such thing as 'a model curriculum' or a 'finished curriculum'. Instead, in **online case studies 4.1 to 4.4, four heads of Department (David Preece, Clare Proctor at East Point Academy, Joseph Milton at Whickham School and Graeme Schofield of Oak National Academy)** articulate the rationale and thinking behind their decision-making in context, describing how they started, evolved and continued curriculum conversations in their schools.

Exploring these examples shows the challenge and diversity of geographical curriculum sequencing. There are few common threads – they don't cover the same topics, case studies or specifications, and have widely different approaches to the use of major conceptual frameworks, geographical enquiry, fieldwork and skills. There are a few topics that are covered by all, but each leader has deliberate reasons for including or excluding others. None of these leaders would claim they had 'the solution' to geography curriculum planning but there is a clear sense that each is solving the problems posed by the opportunities and moments in their context. In many of the reflections, you can also see how curriculum structures evolve – specific examples of trying this one year but moving it the next, or trying one topic only to shift it on finding that it didn't quite work effectively enough.

What I hope you see is a clear rationale, reflection and conversation in building each of these curriculum models. Leaders have appreciated the structure of the subject and the challenges and pragmatic high-level considerations of their context. This means that their curriculum plans are constructed effectively to ensure that students know more, remember more and are able to do more – and achieve the ambitions that their setting and structural opportunities offer. They clearly take their students from a starting point of considering a view of the world and developing a more thoughtful and nuanced worldview through a bespoke teacher-constructed curriculum.

CHAPTER 5
WHOSE GEOGRAPHIES DO WE TEACH?

When we set out to do data collection in fieldwork, we readily accept that we cannot measure everything. We acknowledge that to attempt to get every opinion or measure every sediment piece would be unworkable, and so we make a deliberate and mindful attempt to create a transparent sampling methodology. Doing so acknowledges the gaps that we might have inadvertently left, and recognises the importance of bias, perception and structures that might influence our decision about what to include in our collection, and how good our results and conclusions can be.

But, as we think about the 'construction' or 'contested spaces' of geography in our curriculum choices, we rarely do the same. We make decisions based on incomplete and partial understanding of the world, and our own relationships to it, and we present that to our students and communities as a curriculum. We don't always understand the story behind the curriculum, or the explicit decisions and implicit factors that have gone in to shaping it. And we should, because there are risks if we don't. Some of these might be about what we learn, but other risks are about how we make people feel in our classrooms – whether they feel they are included, belong, and that they and their lived experience are valued as part of what we do.

In Figure 1, we made the disciplinary argument that there is no one route through geography, and that the construction of lesson, case study and curriculum could be contested by others. We must recognise the power of choice, the limits of our choices and the importance of careful consideration when we represent the world around us. Through our language, and our choices, we hold enormous power over the lenses our colleagues, communities and students will go on to develop. We must hold that power carefully and lightly and take time to understand where it sits.

We cannot teach all geography to our students. Even if we ourselves knew it, the scope would require more lifetimes of lessons than we have available. We must therefore make decisions based on the context we work in, the time we have available and the scope of what we know. Pragmatically, we want to do the best job we can with what we've got

– but there are some major academic and human risks that we must be careful to navigate.

Our geography lessons are a small fraction of all that is studied at academic level in the UK, which is a tiny portion of the knowledge through scholarship of all forms across the world. And even those are a tiny percentage of what the world is, and how different people shape and experience it. So why shouldn't we be more transparent about that? What is our 'sampling methodology' for what we choose to teach about the world, and how do we know and communicate it?

Although we can't change the nature of university geography, or the global inequities that we might study, it's right that we think about how we can contribute to the solutions, and how to improve the work of the multiple geographies that make up the modern school curriculum. Some teachers, schools and institutions have already begun to think, talk and act; for others, the discussion is still in the early stages. In some schools, teachers will have complete freedom to choose what they teach; in others, they might be constrained by an exam specification or a centrally developed curriculum. Some schools will be in a community which is particularly affected by challenges: social, demographic or economic. Context matters in this space.

It's important to acknowledge, too, that this is an ongoing conversation – none of us hold all the answers, and that often puts us in a position of discomfort. Based on our own lived experiences, we bring different knowledge, emotion, confidence and privilege to this conversation. Our students and communities might not have teachers who look like them (RGS, 2021) or who can share the lived experience of their community. As a white British, (currently) middle-aged, middle-class cis-male, who was fortunate enough to have the economic privilege and school and parental support network to read geography at university, my lived experience is one without struggle to access my subject, or to find a home and feel that I could belong. I have taught in privileged London schools and found connections in the subject associations and wider communities without difficulty. I am part of the group that Professor Dorling describes as the 'archetypal geography student' (Dorling, 2019). I have little lived experience and insight that I can bring to this space, and I certainly don't have any authority or ability to suggest what the answers might be.

It's fair to say that the nature of this work across the education community means that no one does. But it's right to ask – and keep on asking – the questions, and so this chapter is a series of prompts to help people to reflect on geography's legacy, and the risks we might face in making choices for students in our classroom. Wherever you are in terms of action, conversation or discomfort, it's important that there is an effort to address, educate and counter injustices and inequalities.

While so much of this book builds on the shoulders of geographical giants, I am particularly indebted to the case study contributors for this chapter, who have shared themselves and their stories to give insight into a world that I cannot. Their stories are important – they are likely to be your students' stories too.

What do we mean by 'misconceptions' in geography?

In the Ofsted review (2021), there's a whole chapter on misconceptions, identifying key problems and suggesting solutions:

> *Teachers correct students' misconceptions through secure subject knowledge and effective teaching approaches. They also ensure that their own teaching is accurate and clear. This means that students learn the individual building blocks before moving on to broader composite (or conceptual) knowledge.*
>
> *Teachers respect that in many aspects of geography there is a necessary order to the sequence of learning.*
>
> *Teachers teach content thoroughly without 'corner-cutting'.*

However, a lot of the thinking about misconceptions comes from epistemic disciplines like science or mathematics where there is a justifiable correct answer and there can be understandings which are not correct. That's not true for us. There are multiple geographies, and there are very few lessons where your class is a complete blank slate. In almost every geography lesson, they'll come in with some ideas of their own. These might be:

- **Preconceptions:** Ideas that they have, or perceptions and opinions that exist before you've taught them a topic. These can come from a range of sources including the perspectives of family and friends.
- **Misconceptions:** Ideas and explanations for things that are not correct, that perhaps fit more closely with classic definitions that are more widely used.
- **Alternative conceptions:** Ways of looking at, perceiving or understanding the world that are different to our own or that of the textbook. We need to recognise the importance of plural perspectives

in geography particularly as we seek to diversify and decolonise our curriculum. This is particularly notable in human geography and in decision-making exercises where there is no 'right answer'.

These are a real challenge for you as a teacher. You're not just explaining a concept or topic in isolation: you're also having to work quite hard to think about all the potential ideas and contexts that the students are coming into the lesson with. We are increasingly mindful of false information, and the need for critical reflection and to really be able to trust what you read or find online. Many of these nuances can overlap.

Challenging some of these alternative conceptions might be a direct challenge to people with perceived authority in a student's life. We need to think about how we can carefully and sensitively explore alternative ideas and updated data without causing conflict or challenging relationships. Many of us will have encountered some outdated ideas at parents' evenings when parents explain or express their understanding of geography. Alongside developing your own subject knowledge, Hans Rosling's *Factfulness* (2019) can help you understand how our perceptions of the world can change and how we challenge them, and the Gapminder website (https://www.gapminder.org/) and its 'Upgrade your worldview' tools are worth exploring with your students.

Challenging misconceptions

The suggestions that follow offer ways to deal with misconceptions (in the widest sense) that arise as a result of particular processes.

Students are bringing in wider preconceptions from other sources

Students arrive at school with a wide range of experiences, knowledge and interests, and people around them who share ideas and conversations. It can be the best part of teaching – getting to know your students as people and learning about their aspirations and their world. But it can also mean that you are not their only source of geographical knowledge. They might have read a newspaper article, seen a David Attenborough documentary or a social media clip, or mis-remembered something from a conversation. When addressing this:

- Try to avoid challenging people directly: you don't know where they've learned the information – 'Dad told me, and he's always right'. You don't want to create a conflict so be sensitive to how you share the correction and challenge the misconception.

- Present information carefully and with consideration. We're aiming to develop critical geographers – so they need to understand bias and sources and think about where information is coming from.
- Gently probe the information source. Where did you learn that? How does that fit with what we know? Can we assess the reliability of that?

Students aren't confident with prior knowledge or underlying vocabulary

The easiest way to encounter misconceptions in subject knowledge is to make assumptions about what is already known, or how we use words. Sometimes, we find ourselves in the position of having multiple conversations because people aren't all using a technical word in the same way. This can often happen when there are informal or non-specialist meanings of a word, or when there's popular blurring of lines between words that are clearly distinguished in a geography classroom. A great example of this is the difference between 'weather' and 'climate', and the misconceptions that it can trigger. To address this:

- Ensure 'checking for understanding' is not just procedural compliance. How will you know your students are ready to access the lesson content? Plan to assess pre-requisite knowledge, and use whole-class diagnostic methods (mini-whiteboards, quick feedback mechanisms) to get a quick sense of their current understanding.
- Be prepared to consolidate knowledge if the 'do now' reveals gaps. Don't stick rigidly to your lesson plan at all costs!
- When you're planning, be explicit about what new knowledge is being introduced. Think about vocabulary, concepts, imagery, and how each of these things is being introduced, connected and linked to previous learning. In an ideal world, you should know exactly what and where people have first been introduced to a concept!

There's a plausible distractor

Among the most 'sticky' misconceptions are those which have a logical and plausible alternative explanation. For example, in rivers, it 'feels right' that the river is flowing fastest in the upper course, because we're used to the idea of steep slopes leading to acceleration. The channel efficiency and decreasing friction are less visible, so lots of students are convinced that channel velocity decreases with distance downstream. Misconceptions like these are hard to shift, particularly when we're talking about quite abstract concepts! Try to:

- Use experience and expert subject knowledge to anticipate where the misconception is going to arise from. As you're planning, you can deliberately cue up some key points which start to explore the difference between the idea and the right explanation.
- Think about analogues and explanations that are grounded in concrete examples.
- If you can, set up a live demonstration to make the 'right' explanation just as 'real' as the plausible distractor!

Students feel a need for false balance

People often try to be neutral, and exam specifications may ask students to evaluate by presenting arguments for and against a topic. However, this can lead to misconceptions driven by false balance. For example, scientists are now 'unequivocal' about the causes of recent climate change: they are more than 99% certain it is anthropogenic. To present a 'for and against' in this debate, as if human and physical causes are equally weighted, is to introduce a significant misconception to students. Therefore:

- Look carefully at the evaluations and debates in your teaching (and, perhaps in your own curriculum plans, or specifications), and see what 'balance' is presented?
- What other ways are there to evaluate a discussion or topic? Could you use impacts, scales or some other geographical approach rather than simply a 'for and against' methodology?
- What can we model about excellent balance and evaluation? Where are the best examples of the evidence being presented on this topic?

Clear separation between core and hinterland knowledge

Unfortunately, students are often not the only source of misconceptions. Many can be introduced accidentally through our teaching and lesson planning.

Threshold knowledge is the core content of our subject – transformative, irreversible and the way we move our understanding forwards. *Hinterland knowledge* is the way in which we enable students to access that world. It may be stories, videos or examples that introduce salient points, critiques or places. We need to be mindful of the potential for novice learners to confuse core and hinterland knowledge and privilege the wrong bit! Many of my GCSE students will remember Mike Needleigh, the pig farmer, and his amazing jumpers. Fewer will be able to articulate the aspect of the Holderness case study that his argument illustrated.

Are you telling too many stories, getting distracted by anecdotes? Or, worse, allowing your students to deliberately take lessons off track by asking questions? To avoid this:

- Be explicit about what the required knowledge and processes are at each step. If you do not know what you need to know, how will the students?
- What hinterland knowledge might help? And how might it distract from the core knowledge?
- What specific practice can you include that might help separate core and hinterland ideas in students' minds? Could you ask them to put pens down, or write background information in a different colour?
- Consider time and resources: are you spending more time/energy/attention on the hinterland story? Keep the main thing as the main thing!

Finally, we need to be aware that the geography content itself might lead us to misconceptions in our lessons – particularly when we're using older specifications, textbooks or resources that aren't quite as modern as we might like. Let's have a look at how.

Is our geography accurate?

In a series of powerful TED talks, Swedish Professor Hans Rosling (2006; 2009; 2014) used a data-visualisation platform to clearly demonstrate the difference between popular understanding of inequality and the reality. He focused on economics and development issues and used his well-educated audience to identify popular misconceptions. The platform would eventually become Gapminder (https://www.gapminder.org/), and an associated book, *Factfulness* (Rosling, 2019), critically explored a series of reasons why we might not have the most up-to-date view of the world.

In many cases, it's even harder for us, because of the nature of geography as a rapidly changing subject. While some of the key thinking and theoretical concepts in the discipline may be long-term, the individual examples of places, case studies and information that we use to illustrate them are different almost every day. There are few areas in our curriculum where we can use the same material time and time again without carefully checking to see what's changed or whether it's still relevant. Sometimes, this is as simple as sourcing fresh economic or statistical data but, at other times, the checks might need to be more nuanced as place names, stakeholders and key figures change.

On some issues, the issue of 'accuracy' is further compounded by a question of 'reliability': what sources do we trust will give accurate data about the world and an unvarnished perspective on particular issues? Statistics might contradict each other, use different sampling methods or estimates, or be written at different points in time. New stories and perspectives emerge frequently, giving a challenging perspective on our 'well-known' examples or case studies.

As teachers, we're likely to most strongly associate with the geography that we have been taught ourselves. It's hard to be in direct contact with the cutting edge of research and, while theories might have significantly changed (e.g., Hamill, 2023), we might still be teaching what we know, or what the exam boards 'want us to teach' based on slower evolution of content and specifications. The academic content of university courses may be different to what's in our curriculum, our textbooks or what we learned as geographers.

For example, while plate tectonics theory emerged in 1963, we've had a lot of developments in technology since. Our understanding has changed a lot. A trainee fresh out of a geosciences degree will have a very different understanding of the way that the Earth moves, the driving mechanics of convection currents in the mantle, of ridge push versus slab pull, and a number of more complex debates, to that we knew 10–20 years ago.

There's a challenge here to explore. Do you teach the latest thinking from university level, with the risk of it not being marked as correct in a student's exam? Or do you teach what's specified by the exam board, knowing that it's not the latest thinking? There is no right answer to this, but it's easy to see how students might generate 'misconceptions' and potentially 'inaccurate' answers when being taught by someone whose knowledge post-dates the specification and textbook!

In the case of a changing concept – where teaching at university level might be different to the expected knowledge for a student at KS3, 4 or 5 – this might require a pragmatic conversation about what is the 'best outcome' for your class. The experience of teaching something 'wrong' can be significantly uncomfortable for some teachers. You may want to explore this via examiners' reports, or to address the way in which the conceptual complexity can be explored – but as hinterland knowledge, rather than core. This is a real discussion, and an important one to revisit regularly within your planning.

We also need to pay careful attention to what is being presented as a view – and what is being selected, or omitted – and by whom. In all the textbooks, case study summaries, videos and resources we use in the classroom, someone has made an editorial decision to tell a particular story (Hamill, 2021). They have actively decided to include and emphasise certain things and exclude or not show others. We don't always know what the reasons are – it might be editorial preference, but they can significantly undermine the detail or story of a place. Examples of institutions and individuals moving away from X (formerly Twitter) in response to claims of bias and perception allow us to talk to students about these issues in the pastoral and wellbeing sense – but we ought to do the same with regards to our construction of place, story and understanding events.

Bias by omission is sometimes harder to spot. Roberts (2023: 59) gives examples. Omissions can occur where:

- there is no attention to values or the ethical dimensions of controversial issues
- there is no attention to unequal impacts (e.g., the global dimensions of climate change)
- there is an unequal representation of a diverse place
- there are discussions of patterns or data without an exploration of some significant underlying structural causes or inequalities (e.g., colonial history, legislative arrangements or particular models and theories).

There are plenty of specific examples where this selection and omission causes an inaccurate view of the process, theory or case study being taught. This is a significant area of risk for our geography, but perhaps one which has some measure of quantifiable 'assessment'. A teacher can check the date of the data, or the range of their sources, and be relatively confident that they have made reasonable efforts to overcome these inaccuracies in an objective way.

It is perhaps harder to explore issues of representation which sit within a more constructivist domain, and for us to think about the extent to which the stories that we tell about a place are congruent with the stories that those individuals would tell.

47

Nothing about us without us

'Nothing about us without us' is a slogan which has been used in several contexts to explore the idea that no policies should be decided without the full and direct participation of members of the group(s) affected by it. Originally used as a political slogan in campaigns for democracy and foreign policy, it has been incorporated into disability activism since the 1990s and has since expanded to other movements, including young peoples' health (WHO, 2021) and national, ethic and marginalised groups.

In geography, we might reflect on the extent to which we tell our stories and present ideas. It is unlikely that we will have access to someone from every context, case study location or theoretical space in our curriculum to directly talk to our students. But do we try to explain concepts and ideas in a way that such people would recognise as inclusive and respectful? Do we include their voices – perhaps in multimedia, direct quotes from real people rather than imagined 'cartoons', or in reading and sources – or do we only present our interpretation of what they might think, say or do?

Three structural challenges which might present themselves in our classrooms without this consideration are considered in the rest of this section.

Othering

Drawn academically from psychology and classical studies, the idea of Self and Other – or 'us' and 'them' – is commonly found in literature and considered in historical experiences. However, in social or political contexts, the process can be more critical: reinforcing or creating power imbalances or leading to differentiation, marginalisation or active discrimination and exclusion.

Classical civilisations contrasted themselves with the 'barbarian hordes' – often justifying violent oppression as a moral imperative to bring particular attributes to Other spaces. Through the 19th and early 20th century, Africa was othered in a similar way, with a range of 'expeditions' leading to justifications for imperial conquest. The contemporary post-colonial world is a reaction to imperial demands – empires were often justified and subjugation explained with a narrative of 'civilising', 'developing' or 'modernising' an Other. And, at the time of writing, with the rise of populist politics and increasingly polarised and extreme leadership across multiple countries, the risks of othering as a political and demagogic tool are significant and at the heart of many news stories.

Examples of othering include:

- Representing areas on maps as larger or smaller than they are, so as to distort the relative influence of places.
- Creating an Other which is named and treated as a single, homogenous entity. For example, there is a legacy of presenting 'Africa as a country' (Faloyin, 2022) which reinforces the notion of simplicity and homogeneity. We may also see an Other in terms of development – HICs versus LICs – or when choosing other binary scales that create an implicit 'us and them'.
- Creating an Other which is stereotyped or exaggerated in particular characteristics or scale of threats. For example, the perception of 'immigrants' as a single entity framed as a threat to the British way of life (schools, NHS) in order to create a sense of an external group that has common motives.
- Creating a sense of Self as superior and the Other as inferior – creating a 'need' to solve a problem or act.
- The Other is often marginalised through language choices, perhaps involving core and periphery or insider and outsider perspectives.

It is probably easier and more obvious to acknowledge the spaces where othering takes place in a distinctly racist or discriminatory way, and it's less likely that we would be comfortable teaching an explicit Other in our classrooms. But more difficult to spot is implicit othering as a result of the assumption of white, British, middle-class values or experiences in some sources or perceptions (e.g., tourism topics and expected cultural capital in exam questions), or through consistently presenting particular pathways (e.g., graduate careers), lifestyles (e.g., primary versus tertiary and quaternary jobs) or characteristics as 'us' rather than an Other. Are groups such as the poor, disabled, immigrants or people of different religious, ethnicities or sexualities othered and implicitly 'them' in examples or resources? How alert are we to some of these risks?

Othering clearly causes problems, limits and distortions to our understanding, and whether it's implicit, explicit, or driven by global factors and demagoguery, it's vital that we are aware of our responsibility to identify and take it seriously in geography.

Stereotyping

Stereotyping has some shared characteristics with othering. It reduces a person or a place to 'simplified and exaggerated characteristics' and ignores the potential for nuance or complexity (Hall, 1997). Stereotypes are not necessarily entirely artificial or inaccurate – there is often a grain of truth to begin with – but the reductionist approach renders a complex idea or place too simple.

On the surface, some stereotypes appear relatively harmless. For example, we might assume that 'locals' share an opinion of a management solution, while 'engineers' or 'businesses' take another view. We may even decide to represent these through abstract concept cartoons, or images that are not connected to real places, people or data. However, when we begin to stereotype people or countries, we face a much greater and more significant risk. Stereotypes about Africa (Faloyin, 2022), about 'low-income countries', or about the basis for migration can all be significantly harmful in our classrooms and contexts.

The link to some elements of truth means that these misrepresentations are much deeper and harder to shake. They can influence thinking and inform attitudes because they are not easily dismissed as 'inaccurate' or 'wrong' – and negatively influence our decision-making.

Telling single stories about place

Nigerian novelist Chimamanda Ngozi Adichie (2009) tells the story of how she found an authentic cultural voice in a powerful TED talk, 'The danger of a single story'. Echoing a range of geographical concepts (e.g., Biddulph, 2017), Adichie describes the way that her writing and perception of literature changed when she began to incorporate place-based and culturally authentic themes and experiences.

We can often compound stereotyping and othering structures to generate a single story associated with a place. Adichie describes the 'single story' of Africa as perceived by those she encountered while she was studying in the US – of poverty, catastrophe or pity. She describes the repetitive stereotyping and othering as the creation mechanism of this single story: 'show a people as one thing, only one thing, over and over again, and that is what they become.'

Through case study selection, or by reinforcing stereotypes, we can often accidentally fall into the trap of amplifying or accidentally perpetuating single stories of place. How often do we use Haiti, or Bangladesh, to illustrate vulnerable and disaster-prone areas in direct contrast to higher-income countries who are able to deploy complex protection mechanisms? Do we teach about Bangladesh as more than a place which gets flooded? What do we know about Haiti beyond earthquakes and poverty? How often do we teach about 'slums' (Anderson et al., 2021) and tell a single story about Dharavi, or show the extracts from films or documentaries uncritically? Some of these elements, sadly, are reinforced by specifications, examinations or textbooks – making it harder for individual geography teachers to take a different approach or challenge their students' perceptions.

Like our economic or political structures, or the concepts of othering and stereotyping, the principle of power defines who tells the stories, and how they are amplified. This is almost always a more complex and intersectional challenge than we might first imagine.

In **case study 5.1, Kit Rackley** explores the risk to geography from a personal perspective, where the decisions around inclusivity and inequity are clear to see. We know that the world is a diverse and rich place, and we want to do our best to do it justice.

You need to be alive to the areas and aspects of your curriculum or experience that are potentially stereotyping, othering or inaccurate, and be prepared to change and adapt them. Overcoming the challenges and risks of inaccurate, othered, stereotypical or single-story narratives is made harder – implicitly, explicitly, accidentally and deliberately – by the exercise of power. Our 'sampling methodology' is about more than just representation, it is about systematically understanding the decisions taken to sustain, or perpetuate, particular views of the world, and to explore and understand what and who benefits from that.

Who decides what geography we teach?

We know that geography as a discipline is not a neutral subject. From Eratosthenes 'writing the Earth' in the second century BCE, through the scholars of the Arab world and the Renaissance explorers and cartographers, our discipline was historically powerful in understanding, mapping and shaping our world.

But the use of power is a deliberate decision. The link between geography and imperial ambitions was made in the era of Columbus and the Spanish conquests. Even the legacies of the subject associations are intrinsically tied up in their origins in the service of the British Empire (Livingstone, 1992; Brace & Souch, 2020; GA, 2025). We can acknowledge that Anglo-American geography deliberately contributed to the overseas expansion of empires and that narratives of predominantly white, able, heteronormative supremacy were used to justify it

(Kearns, 2021 and 2021a; Puttick & Murrey, 2021). Colonial and imperial geographies and their contemporary legacies (Anderson, 2021) must be acknowledged, understood and actively countered by fostering a climate of inclusive learning.

The influence of this legacy on our discipline and our professional communities, institutions and the academic subject are an excellent example of the challenging work that is needed to disentangle and recognise the complex issues that academic geography continues to grapple with (Sammar, 2024). It has only relatively recently been given greater prominence in the wider school setting (Lambert & Morgan, 2023; Sinclair & de Fonseka, 2022).

While these issues direct the kinds of content we might study in a curriculum, or might influence the ways our work connects to modern research, in most cases, the decision-making and thinking around this space sits above the classroom setting and teacher agency. The huge issues that geography faces, and the range of challenges posed in chapter 3, shows just how complex these areas can be. Geography can be the study of inequality and the difference in resources and power around the world, but we must recognise that we hold local power as curriculum-makers and teachers (Milner, 2020), and it's often at that scale our efforts and attention are best focused (Milner, Robinson & Garcia, 2021; Reilly, 2022).

How do we go about creating inclusive geography spaces?

Creating inclusive geography classrooms and tolerant classroom cultures requires deliberate effort and intent. You will have a variety of contexts that are determined by your school's environment and wider behavioural cultures, but the way you operate in your classroom will be a key part of the way students feel in your lessons, and how they feel like they are represented or belong in the wider community of school and the subject (Sinclair, 2022). We do not have a blank slate for our geography curriculum – it's important to always site your thinking in your local place and community. The challenges faced by an urban London school may not be the same as those faces by a rural school in Cumbria – and a 'one size fits all' solution to lessons, relationships and curriculum content will probably be appropriate for neither.

Acknowledge and understand your own positionality

As teachers, it's easy to assume that we have knowledge and experience that our students do not. For a lot of our theoretical and conceptual knowledge, it's a safe assumption to make because it is based on our academic qualifications. We may also have professional experience, or wider travel experience, to bring into the classroom.

You will also have values, perspectives, and beliefs about the world – whether they are obvious to you, or not – that shape your thinking and judgements. You will have experiences that have been shaped by your gender, age, sexuality, lived experience of social or economic conditions, upbringing or physical and mental health conditions.

It is important to acknowledge and understand this positionality. There is nothing 'wrong' with having a position – everyone does. Most of them are just about being human and having different viewpoints or opinions on certain topics – they are a world away from deliberate malice, racism or offensive language and statements. But we do need to be aware of them – and of the ways in which they might come out in challenges and influences in our classroom teaching, or relationships with students or parents. (See Table 6 for examples.) Where we know they cause challenges or difficulties, we can plan and deliberately seek to adapt our teaching and language. Where they are unconscious, we may need to reflect, listen and learn about how we can do better.

▼ Table 6: Considerations of positions and potential bias for teachers

Your situation	Consequences for you and your students/ actions to consider
Imagine you have studied science-related A-levels and been a really strong physical geographer at university.	For you, landscapes, processes and quantitative concepts come naturally and easily. It might be difficult to understand why students don't 'get' landscapes on the first explanation.
	Some of your students might be much more afraid of physical geography, or numbers and data.
	Replan. Think about breaking down explanations, so the 'non-physical geographers' can understand and succeed in those lessons (Webb, 2025).

Your situation	Consequences for you and your students/ actions to consider
Imagine your family background was relatively comfortable: you were able to take many field trips at school and go on adventures.	You're concerned that many students don't want to sign up to trips. This may be because they can't afford it, or because they aren't confident being outdoors and doing 'adventurous' things outside their comfort zone. Think about how to make your classroom adventures as enriching as possible. Build up student confidence as they go through the school so older ones are 'ready for residential fieldwork or more ambitious destinations. Plan to support the inclusion of students who face additional barriers, such as those with physical or mental health challenges (see chapter 11).
Imagine you're a heterosexual male teacher, who grew up in a stable family.	In case studies, or examples in, e.g., migration models, you might show images of 'families' as 'Mum and Dad'. The implied message is that heterosexual, two parent homes are 'normal' and everything else is 'other'. Students from a single parent family, or who have two parents of the same gender, might feel alienated, making it harder for them to see themselves in the topics or subject we are studying, and to feel like they belong.
Imagine you studied a classic geography degree at a 'traditional' university.	You are really confident of your knowledge on typical Western geography models, and it's how you select topics, progression and case studies. You find it difficult to understand non-Western geography thinking, or global majority perspectives, and you might struggle to move beyond stereotypical perceptions of globalisation, development or binary narratives. You might even teach evaluative thinking with a bias towards particular solutions (e.g., top-down is successful, HICs always manage events well).

Your situation	Consequences for you and your students/ actions to consider
Imagine you studied geography at GCSE then A-level and then university.	You might automatically assume that this path is necessary for progression into careers with connections to our subject, being unaware of other routes such as apprenticeships. Your students may have experiences or contexts that make this pathway difficult or undesirable. Think about deliberately adjusting language, expectations and the way you talk about certain career paths or progression aspirations.

When it comes to lived experience, and cultural capital, it's important that we recognise the power of the experience our students bring to the classroom. They bring a range of personal and family experience, languages and cultures, and very different perspectives on the world that you can, potentially, use within your lessons and learning. Often, there are no 'right answers', and the perspectives and experiences of our students are likely to be more accurate, more up to date, or more personal than our academic learning. How do we make that come alive, or provide opportunities to talk about it?

Of course, we can't – and shouldn't – insist or expect that students share their lives with us unless we've created a culture where it's safe to do so. To create an inclusive classrooms that makes these moments more likely, you might like to think about:

- How do you create a supportive culture that generates the psychological safety students need to feel confident sharing details from their own lived experience?
- How can you design lessons, activities and moments where cultural capital from students is a welcome addition to the richness of your narrative?
- How can you ensure that your lessons are thoughtfully integrated into the context of your school and environment? How can you meaningfully connect to the wider cultural capital of your location and place?
- How can you build opportunities to let people speak for themselves?

- What can you do to bring in visitors, rich experiences or wider connections to research and scholarship to encourage a geographical curiosity?

Shared cultural capital ensures that we don't make the mistake of telling a single story or giving only one perspective on any place or issue. A short-term, lesson-by-lesson approach will not develop this: it requires a mindset based around classroom culture, and a curriculum that aims to develop, exemplify and deliberately include it over time, as shown in **case study 5.2 by Alice Moy**.

It's clear from Alice's work that the diversity of the curriculum presents an opportunity to show something more, rather than a sense of a 'problem to be solved'.

Move away from deficit model thinking to plural geographies

It's important to work hard to avoid falling in to 'deficit model' thinking where we constantly present our cultural perspective as 'the norm' and anything different from that creates a deficit that we need to 'fix'. Instead, we want to constantly focus on what the individual student can bring, and the ways that these perspectives enrich our classroom and diversity of understanding. Table 7 shows how we might think about the same student contexts in contrasting ways.

▼ Table 7: Examples of deficit and asset model thinking for geography

Deficit model thinking	Asset model thinking
Our students have not travelled much beyond 'their own area': they might not have experience of holidays or multiple destinations they can draw on.	How do we build on our students' really strong connection to place, and to local geographies, and strengthen and challenge their understanding of the world beyond?
Our students have not had significant multicultural experiences beyond their own family background and circumstances.	Our students are deeply rooted in their communities and place. How do we introduce them to other communities in the best way possible?
Our students do not speak English as their first language.	Our students have lots of experiences of the world and cultures that we don't have. How can we bring that in to our work?

Deficit model thinking	Asset model thinking
Our students do not have access to significant learning experiences, or digital resources, at home and may struggle to complete homework or additional tasks.	How do we make the most of valuable lesson time and the resources in the classroom so our students can learn and consolidate/practice at home?
Our students come from communities that don't value geography as much as other subjects.	Our students come from families who have a different perspective on success. We have the opportunity to provide support to help them make decisions about education, higher education and the other pathways available to them – there's lots of potential geographers for us to persuade if we get it right!

So, how can you create an inclusive 'asset model' classroom space?

- Get to know your students as individuals. Learn their names quickly, so you can address them personally and they will be more comfortable and confident to contribute when appropriate.

- Check with students how to pronounce their names – it's important to them that you get it right, but also that you are visibly making the effort to do that!

- Show students that everyone's ideas are valued: create a culture of enquiry and questioning to show that ideas and questions are welcomed and valued; model a culture of discussion and tolerance: be prepared to say 'I don't know that either – let's find out' as a stimulus for scholarship and shared learning.

- Think about the normative language you use – from the way you address the class ('boys and girls' versus 'folks' or 'Year 9') to the examples you talk about in terms of family models, relationships or disabilities. What kinds of images, representation and language will your classes hear throughout their time with you? How can you normalise a tolerant and pluralist perspective in your lessons?

When considering the wider learning experience, and how you might be able to develop learning beyond the classroom, you may want to:

- Explore your department or school policy on the provision of resources for students (e.g., textbooks to take home, photocopies of resources).

- Explore what options are available for onsite support (e.g., after-school homework clubs) if students need to access online materials.
- Consider the extent to which learning tasks outside of the classroom are critical, and how you can bridge the gap where appropriate.
- Explore whether you can use Pupil Premium to provide departmental support for trips and residential opportunities or access to equipment.
- Encourage students to share. Support their development and context with accessible local and relevant examples. Using your local town, or providing really good multimedia or GIS introductions to other places, is good scaffolding for learning!
- Take time to explain options carefully – you cannot assume knowledge of GCSE, A-level or university pathways, or the impacts of decisions. Parents and students alike will welcome this.

It's good practice to carefully consider the assumptions of knowledge and experience that your students have. This is part of planning for misconceptions anyway and helps you to break down knowledge into the smallest steps, but it's also about building long-term relationships with them as human beings. We want to be able to ensure they feel like they belong in our classroom, are represented and included in our curriculum, and can participate and benefit fully from the rich geographical education we can offer.

Make mindful and deliberate decisions about topics and case studies

As geographers, our conceptual and theoretical understanding are usually exemplified through stories about places. Showing videos, using media or reading to tell these stories is a vital part of connecting ideas to real-world examples. The best case studies bring our teaching alive and shine a light on incredible challenges or solutions from around the world.

All too often, in a busy teaching environment, the decisions about what case study to use might be taken for pragmatic reasons (Enser, 2021: 106–108). For example:

- What resources do we have available? Do we have good quality data, images, articles or video clips to use? Have they been professionally quality assured, or are they open to interpretation?
- What is the 'textbook' case study? Although most specifications and curriculum models are rarely precise about individual places to study (although the Sahel is a common example of everyone focusing on the same place), we have textbooks and published materials that tend to

get used regularly. These can be excellent, but over-reliance on them may lead to tired and average answers at GCSE or A-Level – whereas novel case studies might stand out more.

- How old is the case study? Some curricula insist on nothing older than 30 years, which has a philosophically sound reasoning behind it but might leave us searching for examples of specific phenomena (e.g., a significant volcanic eruption in a HIC). There are also risks of 'too soon' for case study use: when an event has just happened, and the impacts – let alone the longer-term impacts – cannot possibly be fully understood or evaluated. 'Classic' case studies may metamorphose in to 'zombie case studies' (Brace, 2024) that are repeated with little evaluation, but there is a deliberate balance in relevance and selection to be struck.

While it's important to acknowledge that some of these pragmatic conversations are important, if we want optimal outcomes, case study selection should be based on the geography: What do we want to exemplify? How do we choose something that represents that well? Once we have established the curriculum topics and areas that we want to cover, we might want to think about:

- How can we use our context and our community to strengthen our place-based understanding and connections? Can we choose case studies from our community and local area?
- How do we deliberately extend our students' understanding of the world? Do we choose connected examples to build on what they already know? Do we want to deliberately expose them to cultural, place or landscape differences?
- Are we using the same case studies for multiple different parts of our teaching? Do we keep coming back to different parts of London to exemplify decline, deindustrialisation, regeneration and rebranding? Do we ask our students to learn twenty case studies, or four or five from multiple angles?
- Are we tying case studies to other elements of our work? We might be able to do a case study of urban decline and use it as a fieldwork example for regeneration. We might be able to investigate our local beach, or river, and use that as a case study of management and impacts.
- Are we linking case studies directly to our developing sense of place? How do case studies fit with each other, and tie together across our curriculum as a whole? How do they sequence and build a more complex or conceptual scheme of understanding of our world?

Try plotting your case studies on a UK and world map. Across your three-year curriculum at KS3, or extending into KS4 and KS5, what is the representation of the world shown?

The deliberate and mindful selection of case studies – to avoid the deficits, and to maximise the assets we have available – is one of the most powerful levers we have to inform and show students what the world around them looks like. It is one that we need to be careful with, and to ensure that we make the right – rather than the easy – choices. We also need to pay close attention to the relevance and accuracy of our case studies and examples – and constantly re-evaluate to understand whether they are still working, still teaching the lessons we want, and still up to date.

How do we keep it all up to date?

Like our curriculum, our case studies and teaching about places should ideally be a continuing conversation between us, our students, and the discipline and the world (see Figure 1). Whereas some of our theories and concepts might be longer-lasting, it's important to look at the ways in which we can explore the accuracy and freshness of our geographical stories, and to make a deliberate plan to update our thinking and examples. Table 8 shows a number of ways to do this at different times and scales.

▼ Table 8: Approaches to keeping our geography up to date

Before teaching a unit of work	Verify links and materials in the work that we're about to teach. Think about checking external video links to see if they still work, or watch them through, to ensure that no new adverts/ inappropriate content have been added since last time!
	Find trusted data sources, and ensure that the data or examples are current and accurate.
	Check that there are no significant changes of context that might make the case study or example limited in relevance.
	Check your student list, and think about whether what you are teaching might have any issues in terms of wellbeing or safeguarding for any of them.
	Reflect on any learning from your previous teaching of this unit – what misconceptions, single stories or things did you have to challenge, and how can you plan to anticipate them this time?

After teaching a unit of work	What misconceptions did your students have? What did they ask or struggle to understand in the first teaching?
	Were there any aspects which caused student or teacher discomfort? What were they? How significant were they?
	Is this something that has been interesting and engaging for students? Were there any notable elements of relevance or challenge? Have other examples come to the fore that might be better?
On an annual or multi-year cycle as a department	What are the key case studies that are being taught across the curriculum, and how do they connect?
	What are the key resources that are being used to teach those examples?
	Are they still relevant? Are they the best possible versions? Are new examples, or new resources required?
	How do you source and reflect on these conversations?
As ongoing professional development	What are the emerging changes in language, concepts or case studies from across the discipline?
	What are the changes in language, concepts or case studies from the examination specifications, reports or reviews?
	How are you developing your ongoing subject knowledge, or engaging with professional reading?

Some of our colleagues may have lesson plans or source material that is unchanged from year to year. However, this work is a vital and valuable part of what makes geography special to teach, and what marks out professionalism as a geography teacher. We are continually learning more about the world – whether that's through updated data, better understanding, or indeed, by professional engagement with further reading and thinking on critical topics.

Any attempt to summarise the complexity of geography as a discipline, or to understand the legacy of power structures, will only ever be a brief overview. It's important that you take time to read and think about the key issues that are represented in your community and context, and in the areas of your own experience and positionality. Some suggestions about where to start are shown in Table 9.

▼ Table 9: Recommended first steps for reflecting on whose geographies we teach

If your focus is	You might like to look at
Understanding how lived experience can impact geography teachers and teaching	Salaam Geographia (https://salaamgeographia.com/) – an excellent resource for the process of tackling uncomfortable conversations and building your confidence with discussing challenging topics. You may also want to look at Sammar's 2024 article based on lived experience.
Understanding how to use authentic voices and sources ethically	Among the great Teaching Geography articles which provide a good insight in to this area from expert practitioners are Habib (2023), Hamill (2021), Kearns (2021a, b), Milner (2020), Milner et al. (2021), Puttick & Murrey (2020), Rackley (2022), Reilly (2022) and Sinclair (2022).
Understanding the wider colonial legacies and issues in geography	The Decolonise Geography community (https://decolonisegeography.com/) have written an introduction to why we need to decolonise geography. Several Teaching Geography articles have explored more conceptual issues, including Anderson et al. (2022); Castree et al. (2023).
Understanding the disciplinary and subject association challenges in equity and inclusion	You might like to reflect and consider who is opting to do your subject (e.g., https://www.rgs.org/schools/geography-for-all project, and Brace & Souch's 2020 report) and the extent which that reflects your school community and your subject. You could read the GA report about diversity and inclusion in the association(GA, 2025).
Understanding how to overcome inaccuracy in data and teaching	Rosling's Factfulness (2019) is the best place to start. You might also like to look at some Gapminder Foundation tools (e.g., https://www.gapminder.org/tools/ and https://www.gapminder.org/dollar-street).

Subject associations, teachers and academics are continuing to do significant work in this space, and this list will undoubtedly grow through time. It is important to remember that we are all on this journey, and all our classrooms offer plenty to learning and reflection on. Please be part of the discussion and put it in action!

CHAPTER 6
HOW DO WE CREATE CHALLENGE IN THE GEOGRAPHY CLASSROOM?

The concept of 'challenge' in the geography classroom serves as a useful bridge between the curriculum-making conversations of the previous chapters and the lesson planning conversations of the chapters to follow. Ultimately, 'challenge' is the level at which we pitch our lessons, and how we build and sequence our content and skills to develop students' understanding of the world around them.

One of the components that makes geography an amazing subject is also one of the biggest challenges we face when predicting what students will struggle with: everyone – whether teacher or student – has their personal perceptions, preferred topics and things they find more challenging to explain or to understand. This is also one of the reasons why progress in geography is so challenging to measure. We've all met an amazing student who suddenly appears to be go backwards at KS4. And it's not because they've suddenly become less excited about geography, or stopped engaging with lessons; it's simply because they've encountered a topic that is less familiar, less comfortable or comes less naturally to them. So, when we talk about challenge and 'difficulty', we should acknowledge that it's a very personal, and often very variable term.

Identifying threshold & difficult concepts

Perhaps more useful for us as teachers, then, is to think about ideas that are so fundamental to our subject that students are unable to make progress if they're not secure in their understanding of them. Meyer & Land (2003) refer to the particular knowledge that is key to student progress as 'threshold concepts'.

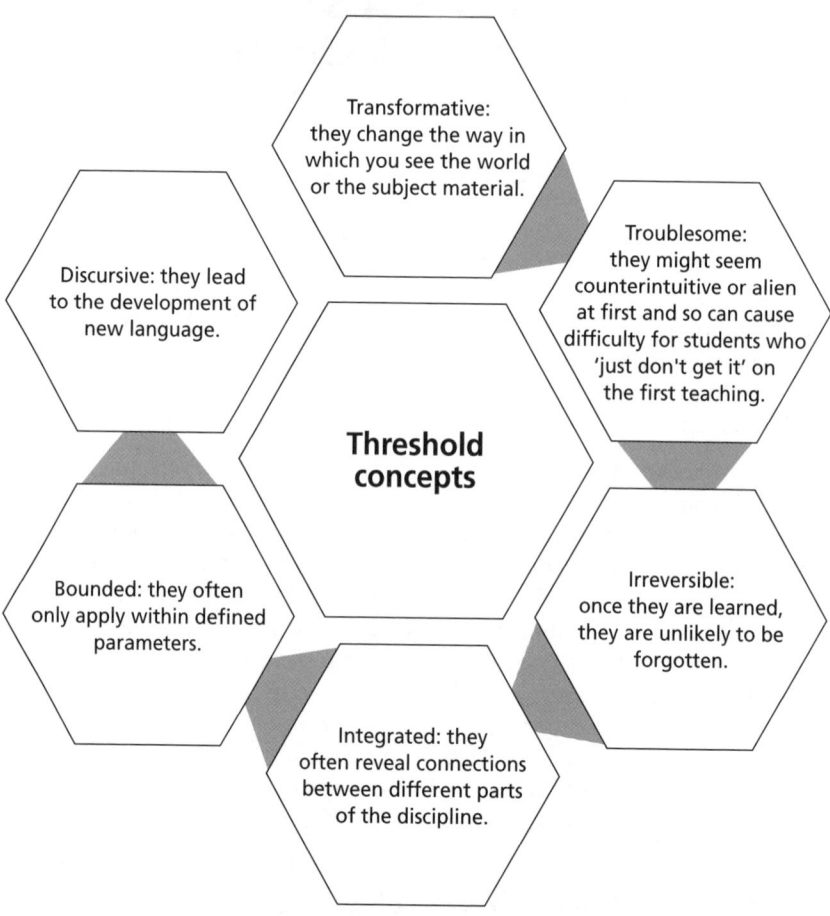

▲ Figure 4: Threshold concepts (Meyer & Land, 2003)

We work with threshold concepts all the time, and many of them are specific to an individual topic. For example:

- the concept of longshore drift underpins many coastal topics
- the concept of plate movement underpins many hazards topics
- the model and concept of global atmospheric circulation underpins a significant number of physical and human topics.

However, a number of threshold concepts that we encounter in geography are about a way in which we perceive the world. For example, younger students may struggle to understand how to perceive a three-dimensional space in a two-dimensional representation, and to see how the world and the globe can be directly linked to map projections or images.

In physical geography, we often represent place and time interchangeably. For example, we will draw diagrams that show multiple stages of the evolution of a landform as if they are occurring at the same place next to each other – the classic 'cave → arch → stack → stump' sequence is a great example of this. Students can sometimes struggle to understand the coherence between a diagram showing the conceptual progression of a landform formation, and images, sources or maps which show those landforms at different isolated moments in time. We also see this in the progression of weather: it's quite common for people to think that rain starts or stops in a particular location, rather than appreciate the transformative idea that a pressure system is moving over an area.

The concept of time – and geological time in particular – is another key threshold concept for students. For a significant number of topics, it is only when we are able to step outside the period of human existence that we can understand how rivers, glaciers or climate change truly have power over our landscape. But this is an abstract and quite challenging concept to explore and explain in isolation, and needs to be revisited and applied often to ensure that it 'sticks'.

It's important, then, to consider threshold concepts in our medium-term planning. We need to be confident that we can identify what they are, and where students first encounter them. As a team of teachers, we need to get comfortable that we all agree on the same definition of what the threshold concept is, and how we teach, sequence and explain that best. Once we have done that, we need to think about how our students have frequent opportunities to explore, or to check their understanding, of them. For example, we might:

- **Use them to design and structure our curriculum.** Geography lends itself to different curriculum models, and many people favour the idea of a spiral curriculum where threshold concepts are taught and revisited often.
- **Use them when planning a sequence of learning.** We may wish to use our sequence of learning to identify the waypoints at which we introduce threshold concepts. For example, we could start with a threshold concept and then explore its impact, as we may do with the concept of geological time. Alternatively, we could build up to

a threshold concept, which then unlocks further implications in the second part of a unit of work. You could do this with the global atmospheric circulation, for example, where the introduction of the model allows you to develop a greater understanding of the impacts on people of a specific weather event or biome.

- **We need to make sure that students are secure in threshold knowledge before moving on**, so we need to identify who has gaps and where. You may sometimes see these referred to as hinge questions. We also need to think about how we close these gaps. There is no point moving on through a lesson plan if a student has a fundamental misunderstanding of, or misconception about, threshold knowledge.
- **Revisit often in different contexts or using different approaches or sources**. For example, if we've taught the global atmospheric circulation model in a weather topic, we may want to come back to it at the start of a unit of work on biomes, or at the start of the unit of work exploring regional variants across the African continent. This allows students to demonstrate the links between the different parts of the discipline, to use the language and discursive components that they have previously been taught, and to build a synoptic and connective approach towards a deeper understanding of the topic.

Identifying controversial and wicked problems

> A geography curriculum that disregards values and controversy would not only be very dull (and also very thin in terms of content), but more importantly would fail to educate.
>
> (Biddulph et al., 2015)

There's never been a time where the importance of a geographical understanding is more obvious. The interconnected world in which we live demands a complex and nuanced view, but it also exposes us to different cultures, contexts and ideas. Our subject presents students with real issues – global and local – and encourages them to think about their perspectives.

But these issues can become controversial or become the subject of different guidance and opinions. Wherever there is no fixed or universally held perspective, there's room for debate, perception and opinion. Roberts (2023: 109–111) suggests that issues are controversial for different reasons, which need to be explored as part of our thinking:

- **There is insufficient evidence.** Sometimes decisions must be made around a range of environmental or scientific or management issues even when the evidence is still insufficient or uncertain.
- **There are differences of interpretation.** We recognise plural perspectives and should be confident in the fact that there are multiple geographies and multiple truths on issues like these.
- **There is a conflict of values.** Stakeholders are often influenced in their viewpoints by the relative priority they give to environmental, economic, social, cultural or political considerations. This is particularly evident when we talk about management decisions, where views are related to which of the considerations or values are highest priority. It's also important to acknowledge that decisions are informed not just by factual evidence and the strength of arguments from different value positions, but also on the relative power of groups to influence outcomes.
- **There is a conflict of ideologies.** Opinions are often underpinned by ideological assumptions: for example, a particular belief or way of thinking about economic policy. Different approaches may be more implicit than explicit and often need to be unpicked carefully.
- **NIMBYism.** Often, people are in favour of an approach in principle, but will reject it if it is proposed in their local area. This is referred to as NIMBYism ('not in my back yard'). Several decision-making exercises and management case studies show clear evidence of people's opposition based on local visual, noise, traffic, access or ecological impacts, and these are good examples of how students can learn the local importance of particular perspectives.
- **Ethical reasons.** Many of the controversial issues that we face have ethical dimensions. Setting an ethical decision against a cost–benefit analysis, or treating an ethical reason as different or somehow superior to alternative conceptions for a proposal can generate significant controversy in the classroom. Examples involving migration, religious perspectives or expansion related to neocolonialism often offer ethical dimensions to an issue to be explored.

As an alternative to framing problems as 'controversial', we may prefer instead to explore 'wicked' or 'super-wicked' problems in a disciplinary or academic sense. The term was originally introduced to describe town planning problems:

Planning problems are inherently wicked as distinguished from problems in the natural sciences which are definable, separable and may have solutions that can be found. The problems of government planning – and especially those of social or policy planning – are ill defined; and they rely on elusive political judgement for resolution.

(Rittel & Webber, 1973: 160)

Rittel & Webber identified ten distinguishing properties of these problems, and the term is now commonly used by policy makers and academic geographers.

▲ Figure 5: Properties of 'wicked problems' (after Rittel & Webber, 1973)

Kelly Levin and colleagues developed this further arguing that urgent or important problems were 'super-wicked' in cases where:

- time is running out
- the central authority needed to address them is non-existent
- those who caused the problem seek the solution
- responses can be pushed into the future.

As an example, climate change has been described as 'arguably the most super-wicked problem of our times' since there is a need for 'forward reasoning' and scenario-building to consider alternative futures and move towards preferred outcomes (Lazarus, 2009; Levin et al., 2012). We may equally consider conflict in the Middle East or Russia as examples of super-wicked problems.

Effective approaches to teaching controversial topics

Whether you choose to frame them as controversial or wicked, it's important that problems should be fundamentally geographical in nature, and should clearly identify the geographical content and concepts to be taught. This helps us to differentiate from ethics debates in RE, for example, and can potentially reduce and mitigate potential concerns from parents or students. Issues where there is a conflict of interest between different groups are commonly used; these can range from local planning issues to national projects such as Heathrow Airport expansion or the Three Gorges Dam in China. It's important that you choose the case study with care – both in terms of relevance, but also in terms of providing a range of sources and perspectives that allow for positive and appropriate geographical debates. Some discussions may feel relevant in the present moment, but the wider perspective and true understanding may not emerge for some time. There is always a tendency to try to teach towards current events rather than well-established case studies – but there are risks involved in that approach, and you should judge carefully!

If you're looking to identify potential areas in the curriculum, Roberts (2023) suggests that you consider:

- Topical issues – local, national, or global – that are in the news. Be aware that you may not know the full picture of a 'current event' – and it could easily take a difficult and challenging turn!
- Local issues, where you might find easy access to information from local newspapers, or the planning department, and you could involve local people as visitors or through questionnaire surveys.
- Issues you know about through study or travel.
- Geographical issues of particular interest to the class or context. Schools in coastal areas may look at the management of areas like theirs; schools in urban contexts might explore regeneration or community issues that are a direct contrast or in comparison to their own. If there's a space to learn from another similar region, and apply to a closer and more local context, that can be very powerful.

Controversial issues are invariably complex, and it can require a breadth of geographical understanding to grapple with them. Beware of dealing with issues in a single lesson, or on a very superficial basis. This can be a particular problem at KS3, where an issue may be over-simplified in an attempt to make the topic accessible for all students. Good curriculum sequencing is important here – both in terms of pre-existing knowledge, but also in terms of where the controversial or challenging component comes within a medium-term plan. At the lesson scale, it's usually best to do the complex decision-making work at the end of a unit of work – so students have built up knowledge, and understanding, before making judgements and decisions. At the curriculum scale, it's important to recognise the sequencing of prior knowledge that makes sense of ideas.

It is common for climate change to be explored at KS3, for example. But how often do we see that as part of a fully sequenced idea of learning, which sets in the wider context of global atmospheric circulation, the differentiation of weather and climate, and *then* the factors of climate which create change? If we teach 'climate change' before students have a decent understanding of the weather and climate that has historically been expected, we run the risk of creating isolated pockets of misconceptions and challenges for later!

It's important that we teach our students that the world is complex, and that there are situations with no simple answers. But it's also important that we understand our role in this learning, and to be clear about the extension of 'subject matter' into cognitive, affective or emotional domains. For lots of people, the chance to shape the lives of young people is a key motivation for becoming a teacher, but we should do that sensitively and with consideration to our values and how they align. Table 10 shows a range of different ways that values can be explored in our classroom.

▼ Table 10: Approaches to values education (Lambert & Balderstone, 2000: 293)

Values inculcation	Has the objective that students will adopt a predetermined set of values
Values analysis	Uses structured discussion and logical analysis of evidence to investigate values issues
Moral reasoning	Provides opportunities to discuss reasons for value positions and choices with the aim of encouraging growth of moral reasoning ability
Values clarification	Aims to help students become aware of their own values in relation to their behaviour and that of others
Action learning	Encourages students to see themselves as interacting members of social and environmental systems through having them analyse and clarify values with the intention of enabling them to act in relation to social and environmental issues

It's easy to see how a range of teaching approaches – and perhaps even an ethos of a school – could fit within one or more of these value approaches. You may have a particular perspective that fits within one approach. As a teacher, your values are important, but it's key that you work within the guidance of the profession, and your school's own policy.

In planning the effective teaching of controversial issues, Fry (2018) suggests that teachers:

- Clarify their own values and decide what stance they will take on the issue. This is also a good time to consider and confirm wider school stances or policies which might influence decision-making by the teacher.
- Consider the complexity of the issues and how they will approach this appropriately for the class they are teaching.
- Identify clear aims and learning outcomes for the unit of work.
- Decide what teaching approach will be most appropriate with this class and topic.
- Decide what resources and supporting material will be most appropriate for this class and topic.
- Select active learning strategies that give plenty of opportunity for discussion of different opinions. What prior conditions of debates, discussions and 'ground rules' might you need to have scaffolded before you get to the controversial topic?

Students will bring their own opinions and ideas to geography lessons, and this is to be encouraged. But, because they will also bring with them ideas from parents, peers, social media and other lessons, which sometimes display prejudice and stereotypes, teaching about controversial issues requires carefully selected resources and consideration of the relationships you have with a class.

It's important to think about the skills that students need to be able to emotionally and behaviourally cope with challenging lesson content, rather than solely considering the academic or curriculum thinking. You may wish to decide the extent to which there should be a substantial element of student discussion, so they can discuss ideas with others, clarify values and form opinions. It is easier to do difficult topics with lots of discussion later in the year, once your classroom culture and behavioural routines are firmly established, rather than the first half term when you're still getting to know the students! You may want to plan activities where you:

- adopt a neutral role by being an impartial chairperson for a discussion
- state your own position openly so that students know where you stand
- take a balanced approach presenting a wide range of alternative views
- be a devil's advocate – which can enliven discussion.

There are some components of anticipation, and perhaps even deliberate preparation, that might help you build confidence too:

- How will you encourage students to think critically about the issues? What specific questions, structures or key perspective shifts can you use to support that?
- How will you deal with individual students/groups who may present challenges? Who are the specific students that you might want to cater for? What do you anticipate being their particular needs, and how do you support them?

A geography curriculum inherently needs to tackle difficult topics and decisions to do justice to the subject (Hesslewood, 2021). These areas, where there is no clear right answer, can feel intimidating to teach and challenging to plan for. However, with careful consideration, there is no reason to fear them. They should be part of an authentic and representative curriculum, of great geography lessons.

CHAPTER 7
HOW DO WE PLAN GREAT GEOGRAPHY LESSONS?

Mode A and Mode B teaching were originally introduced as part of Sherrington's *The Learning Rainforest* (2017), which explored the variations between the common direct instruction approaches to teaching (Mode A) and the more subject-specific or rarer kinds of lesson activity, which offer a wide and varied diet of learning activities for awe and wonder (Mode B). While Sherrington advocates a ratio of Mode A/Mode B of about 80/20, we need to acknowledge the practical and pragmatic tensions in some of those spaces.

Mode A teaching

A significant portion of Mode A teaching is based on the principle of the gradual release model (Table 11), and it's important to think carefully about the various steps involved in that sequence.

▼ Table 11: Graduated modelling approach for teachers

Stage	Teacher	Students
I do	Provides a carefully sequenced explanation or demonstration of the task. Likely to lead or model from the front of the classroom, using tools if appropriate.	Are focused on the teacher's explanation, and likely to be doing little individual work or discussion. Check for understanding of the teacher explanation through questions, rather than activities.

Stage	Teacher	Students
We do	Provides a scaffolded or sequenced activity to allow students to create their own version of the task or activity. Likely to be highly chunked and carefully sequenced – small actions, followed by a check for understanding and conceptual comprehension. Likely to have a 'good example' that is now shared in teacher space (board, visualiser) and student space (books, notes, mini-whiteboards).	Are involved in the task or activity in their own notes, books or space. Are working through the activity and engaged in completing the task at each stage of the instruction. Are going to be listening, then working, then checking, then listening to the next sequence.
You do	May circulate to provide support and guidance to students individually to complete the activity or task. Is not providing new information, unless whole-class misconceptions are identified, in which case we start again.	Students working individually in their own learning space (e.g., book, booklet, mini whiteboard, computer) to complete the activity. Likely to have longer periods of silence or low teacher input.

We should remember that the gradual release model is designed for learning, not to be a complete cycle of learning all the way through to assessment. Each of these stages is about taking on board new information, not necessarily directly jumping to assessment of knowledge.

It's also important to think about how we make this a specifically geographical experience. Roberts (2011) has identified these three essential aspects of a good geography lesson, shown in Table 12.

▼ Table 12: Essential aspects of a good geography lesson (Roberts, 2011)

Teaching connects with students' minds and prior learning	The geography teacher should pay attention to: • supporting all students' learning and progress, which includes adaptive teaching and clearly modelling for all to access the learning • eliciting what students already know and understand about the geography • checking and correcting misunderstandings, or anticipating misconceptions • finding out students' opinions and feelings where appropriate.
Geography is included	The geography in a lesson will be represented by at least one of the following, and it may include all of these: • Geographical data. This includes maps, visual data of all kinds, statistics, graphs, text, etc. It can be in textbooks, on resource sheets, through presentations or on the Internet. Students need use geographical data to help them understand the complex world in which we live. • Geographical ideas. These may be generalisations, concepts, theories; and they should underpin the lesson. • Locational context. Students should know the location of the places they are studying and their significance. Teaching provides opportunities for students to make sense of the geography.
The teacher	The geography teacher will: • Give students time to explore new geographical information and relate it to what they already know. • Allow students to discuss ideas and geographical data with each other and the teacher. • Ask for consolidation and extended writing so that students need to sort out geographical information and ideas and make links between them.

It's important to understand the principles of the thinking here. This isn't a checklist for every single lesson. It's entirely possible that in an individual lesson there'll be more focus on one of these components than others – or that there will be some parts missing. That's normal.

Learning happens over a long time: it's not magically aligned to 45-minute or 60-minute blocks because your timetable is written that way. So, we might see some of these components over a longer learning journey, and need take our curriculum mindset to a medium-term plan.

> ### Critical reflection
>
> It is worth being pragmatic about the balance between Mode A and Mode B. While many of us would love to have a range of other activities regularly embedded within the daily Mode A diet of our lessons, the challenges of resource access often means that we may not be able to do them as frequently as we want. For example, there is an inherent tension between the ways that we *might like to teach* using regular opportunities to embed GIS or directly related small-scale field work activities, and the reality of a timetable, or lack of IT resources which make this difficult on a lesson or termly basis.
>
> And so, a number of our desirable activities become de facto Mode A lessons, *primarily* because we do not have the ability to access them as regularly as we would like. In some cases, we can modify those by 'teaching from the front' or offering virtual trip solutions, but we know these are substitutes for what we really want to do, or what we believe will offer the deepest learning. This does not mean that we regard them as additional or optional activities, but is simply a recognition of the situation in many schools and classrooms.

How does Mode A apply in geography?

The range of geographical knowledge required to make synoptic links is considerable, and much of it is abstract or based on expert schema and teacher subject knowledge. The most effective way to provide students with building blocks of knowledge is to explain it carefully and deliberately in a way that ensures that the new information is retained (Sherrington, 2019). Although each piece of information might be quite simple, it's our job as teachers to ensure that we think carefully about how we are placing each piece of information into the larger picture, so that students can start to build up and develop schemas of understanding and geographical skills appropriate to their developing level of expertise.

The teacher needs to be in control of the individual explanation, as well as understanding how it is fitting into the development of a mental model. There are a number of wider theories of learning and cognitive load which help us to form reference points for how these explanations may best develop student thinking. In particular, the key ideas of dual coding, cognitive load theory, and Mayer's theory of multimedia learning (Mayer, 2020) give guidance to the sequence and thoughts that may support teachers planning for their explanation. Tayler (2024: 9–12) shows how a number of these key principles can be applied to lesson design, slide and diagram design in order to effectively sequence explanations for learning. These expert explanations also need to be really focused on the threshold concepts and intentions of the lesson – there is no point delivering an amazing explanation that does not support your direction of curriculum travel, or that sits outside of the existing knowledge and sequence for your students.

At each stage, it's important that you remember you are in control of the flow of knowledge. You need to chunk the key ideas into manageable parts, which direct and regulate:

- **The flow of information from teacher to student.** If a teacher is actively engaging the class, checking for understanding, and live-correcting misconceptions, they can pause and revisit areas of an explanation as they need to. You might sometimes hear this referred to as the 'pace' of a lesson – when there is more information than the students can cope with at a particular point in time, the lesson will 'feel too fast'; when most students have more time than they need to process information or complete a task, the lesson will feel slow.

- **Students' attention and priorities.** It's important that students are directed to the most important parts of a diagram or a sequence of information. Unless we strip back geographical ideas, we are always likely to have lots of complications or nuances to explore. As a teacher, part of the job of your explanation is to focus students on the relevant bit at the right time!

The management of this involves a curriculum mindset and being conscious of the prior learning (concepts, processes, landscapes and landforms, specialist vocabulary, places or specific case study knowledge) that is required to make the most of the learning in this moment. **You can see how this works in case study 7.1 by Abdurrahaman Perez-McMillan of the Harris Federation.**

Good geography explanations

Having planned and considered how to chunk subject knowledge carefully, and created the curriculum and classroom conditions for learning, you need to be able to consider how best to teach your explanation in the classroom setting.

Drawing diagrams

Diagrams are a really key component of good instruction in geography. We need to think carefully about how we present them – not just in terms of the subject matter, but also how we take time to build them up and model their construction for our students (Powell, 2023). It's worth considering:

- How do you choose to present the information? A picture? A constructed diagram on a board or under the visualiser?
- Do you present a complete example first, and then build it up together ('I do', 'we do')?
- How do you ensure that students understand what they are looking at (e.g., being really explicit about 'this is a top-down view', or 'this is what it looks like from the side') and how to interpret the diagram (e.g., 'this is what it evolves to over time, but I'm going to just draw them next to each other so you can see').
- How do you make sure that the diagram is accessible in your classroom? Can it be seen from everywhere? What colours are you using? How do people read it from the back of the room?

Drawing great diagrams is a real skill that is developed, practised and built up over time. You shouldn't be afraid to rehearse and build your confidence, or to learn from others.

> **Reading recommendation**
>
> Luke Tayler's excellent *Visualising Physical Geography* (2024) provides a structured and thoughtful introduction to the purpose, nature and techniques involved in drawing diagrams for physical geography. Through the first chapters, the theories of cognitive loading and multimedia principles are explained, and the steps towards careful and detailed explanation are modelled clearly. If you are looking for a great primer on how to teach well, not just in developing diagram confidence or subject matter expertise, this is the book to read.

Using technology

Technology can enhance the relevance and authenticity of our teaching and learning. When you are planning to use it, you need to begin with the end. You need to be clear how the use of technology comes from the learning needs. Think about how it could improve learning and how it will supplement and enhance teaching (EEF, 2021) rather than just being 'an experience' or a 'shiny toy' to play with. It can be a valuable resource in supporting engagement, allowing multiple means of representing information and, therefore, wider access to learning. It can also allow students to demonstrate their knowledge and understanding in ways beyond traditional 'pen and paper' written assessments.

Appropriate technology you might use includes:

- Videos to introduce new content.
- Visualisers to project worked examples.
- Instructional apps – apps that provide instruction, modelling, or practice opportunities for a wide range of skills.
- Non-instructional apps – apps that provide tools to aid learning, such as note-taking apps.
- Assistive technologies, such as speech-generating apps to augment the communication skills of students with communication difficulties.

While most of these tools have been used in lessons for a while, the visualiser is a relatively recent introduction to the technological landscape that has had a massive impact on geography lessons. As well as being used for teacher demonstrations, or live modelling, you can also use it to demonstrate student examples – whether that's great practice, or shared drafting of ideas that the whole class can then develop further. **Extras 7.1 gives some guidance on using a visualiser.**

Explaining places and case studies

Once you have chosen your case studies, or placed examples, as part of your curriculum planning, introducing them and explaining the relevant learning points is a key part of Mode A teaching. It's important that you consider the following questions:

- How will you contextualise the location and geography of the case study or place? Where does it sit within the country/context, and how do you demonstrate zooming in from a larger scale?

- What multimedia do you have available to deepen understanding of the place or case study? How can you use other tools (e.g., GIS) or resources to show multiple dimensions or nuances of the case study?
- How up to date is your data, and how recently did you check it?
- What are the key pieces of information – facts, figures, learning points, conclusions or analytical perspectives – that are most critical to students for this case study?
- How do you encourage students to spend time in the geography and make sense of information – what are you doing to explore skills, analysis or wider processes of being a good geographer?
- How do you separate core content from hinterland content, and enable students to focus on the former?
- How do you remind students about the diversity and representation themes of the curriculum decisions, and avoid the single-story narrative?

Clear understanding of a case study or place comes from a thoughtful and sequenced explanation of it, and it's important that the detail of case study learning points are just as carefully taught as other aspects of theory or instruction! You can see an example of this thinking in **case study 7.2 by Brendan Conway of Notre Dame School.**

Modelling

Modelling is one of the most powerful tools in a teacher's toolkit, and fulfils a range of purposes within the geography classroom. At all stages, the key role of modelling is to make visible the thought processes and domain-specific expertise of the teacher, and invite students to understand the geography, thinking and processes behind the activity.

In terms of the gradual release model, it is most commonly linked to the 'I do' and 'we do' phases of teaching, but it can also be a powerful reflection and evaluation process for the 'you do' stage. Showing students what we'd look for, or how we could improve existing answers is an important part of closing that feedback loop, and a helpful reminder about the importance of both parts of the work!

The sections below discuss what are, perhaps, the three most critical areas to be modelled in a lesson.

To enable students to engage with content

This is a common element of the gradual release approach and may also overlap significantly with aspects of explanation. For example, we might see:

- Modelling answers or solutions to 'do now' activities or early questions.
- Drawing diagrams and modelling completion or labelling as part of an explanation phase.
- Modelling the use of vocabulary or terminology during instruction.

To enable students to engage with disciplinary thinking and techniques, including geographical skills

This is one of the most important components of modelling for teaching, and in building a disciplinary mindset in students. Modelling and 'walking–talking' examples are not just about exam skills or application of knowledge, but a real way to verbalise and make concrete some of the invisible schema of our expert knowledge and understanding. Good examples of modelling in this space include:

- Demonstrating how to use or interpret geographical information, like annotating a photograph or sketching a landform.
- Modelling the annotation and interpretation of text or sources.
- Modelling the construction or analysis of geographical data, graphical information or sources, or the completion of numerical or statistical analysis tasks.
- Modelling the use of GIS.
- Modelling the use of mind or concept mapping to break down a topic or question.
- Modelling the use of revision techniques or learning techniques.

Understanding geographical thinking is a fundamental part of the modelling process: students need to be able to see how someone else identifies key features, or draws connections together in a synoptic way.

To enable students to write and express their ideas in a more fluent or geographical way

This is probably one of the areas where modelling is most often used, and is common to a number of disciplines. We are more comfortable with the concept of modelling writing, or modelling exam answers, and students will likely have seen it done across multiple subjects. They might have seen examples of someone:

- Annotating a question, or starting to plan thinking or essay structures based on a prompt.
- Writing a model paragraph structure, or annotating an example paragraph to highlight the structural features.
- Annotating an essay to show the structural features.
- Writing exam answers, or annotating exam questions to show the marking or structural features of a response.
- Annotating written responses to show a particular development strand (e.g., highlighting and focusing on subject-specific vocabulary, or an evaluation strand etc.).

We can also consider the extent to which we only model 'good' examples and how those are sourced and derived. It can be really powerful to amplify good work by having students show it under the visualiser as a 'model', but some students might find that difficult. It would take a significant investment in classroom culture and trust to be able to use student work as examples of 'what not to do' without damaging the students' self-confidence, and it's often easier to generate your own 'what a bad one looks like' example if that's an important aspect of what you want to model.

However, it's important to acknowledge that not all students will be able to do the modelled work on their first attempt without additional support. This is where scaffolding becomes important as part of Mode A teaching.

How can you scaffold learning?

As in our modelling, there are a number of different reasons why we might scaffold learning in a particular way. The purpose of a scaffold is to support transition from 'I do' through 'we do' to 'you do', and they should be temporary structures that occur at a range of scales. It does not have to look the same for all students at the same time, and we might combine multiple scaffolds in the same lesson or activity. For example, over a unit of work we might have universal 'diamond nine' scaffolds and paragraph structures that are slowly withdrawn as we teach evaluative essay writing skills, working alongside individual vocabulary or word mats and structure strips for specific and targeted student needs.

You may find that you develop departmental or whole-school approaches to scaffolding. The consistency of these can be a real confidence booster and support to students, but we need to think about whether they are achieving the right outcomes for geography. The way they structure a data analysis task in science might not be suitable for us; and our English colleagues might not write paragraphs that universally apply to how we want to communicate!

Often – whether deliberately or not – a number of scaffolds reflect how we want our students to work under assessed conditions, and they might reflect particular variances of exam specifications or even the marks available for a typical question style. It is common to see memory-jogging acronyms scribbled in the margins of exam papers, or supplied in mock exams as student prompts. It's important that you consider which scaffolds are right – not just for your students, but also for your wider context – and critically evaluate how to apply some of the ideas.

To enable students to engage with content

There are a number of ways that scaffolds can be used to support and develop student thinking about geography content. For example:

- Spider diagrams/mind maps/concept maps used to introduce, scaffold or encourage the development of synoptic thinking and links between different areas of a topic or concept.
- Layers of inference diagrams or scaffolded annotation approaches used to introduce and scaffold ways of exploring images or sources and generate interpretative ways of thinking.
- Teaching mnemonics or structures to learn approaches.
- Scaffolds to get students thinking about how to describe data or a pattern on a map. For example, we could use TEA (trend – the overall pattern; evidence – quote something from the data, source or map; anomaly – check if there's anything that doesn't 'fit' the overall trend) or HLTA (highest – the highest data point; lowest – the lowest data point; trend – the overall pattern; anomaly –anything that doesn't 'fit'), both of which work really well in supporting students to think about sources and images/maps. Again, teachers might choose one or the other of these, depending on the structure of their GCSE exams – if you have 3 mark 'describe' questions, then TEA works, but HLTA works really well if you have 4-mark questions!

To enable students to engage with disciplinary thinking and techniques, including geographical skills

There are several specific scaffolds for geographical skills, which we will look at in later sections. As well as the ability to connect and link ideas in a synoptic way, one of the key disciplinary approaches that we often need to scaffold is the development of evaluative thinking, and being comfortable with multiple criteria for success judgements.

It is common to see some variation of diamond nine grids used to develop this. A 'diamond nine' grid is a square of boxes, rotated to give a diamond shape – and it can be pre-prepared or simply sketched or generated ad hoc in lessons.

When asked to give a linear 'most important to least important' ranking factor decision, students can agonise over which factors are at the same level, or with different contexts etc. By providing a scaffold where there is one 'most important' and then others at 'important' and 'less important' layers, we move away from a rigid mindset to encourage more nuanced thinking, and the sense of 'it depends' that characterises synoptic and disciplinary approaches to geography.

This kind of scaffold can often work at multiple levels – helping students not just organise their understanding or learning about a concept, but also their ability to express that information more clearly in a spoken or written response.

To enable students to write and express their ideas in a more fluent or geographical way

A significant number of scaffolds operate to ensure that students are able to express their ideas more confidently – either in terms of the quality of their written output, or in the quality of the geography they are including.

At the simplest level, some students require support to access the more complex vocabulary that geography requires. Having a word mat – a sheet of key vocabulary, main terms, or Tier 2/3 vocabulary – might help individuals access the lesson content.

As we start to write more, it is common to see some kind of paragraph scaffold being taught. Some students find the idea of a scaffold structure for paragraphs really helpful but they each have relative advantages and disadvantages, and they can often be limiting for great students, who can express their geography better. Scaffolds may overlap with those used by colleagues in, for example, English, History or RE and it can support the development of consistency if you can have a similar approach to other departments. It's down to the department or school to try and put a collective strategy in place so that as many subjects as possible get the most out of it! Common paragraph scaffolds include:

- **PEE**: Point – Evidence – Explanation: designed to get students to simply think about what they want to say, and how they support that with further perspectives, potentially including case study evidence.
- **PDL**: Point – Develop (Discuss) – Link: designed to make a point, develop it (perhaps with evidence) or extend and show the limits of the point in a discussion, and then link to the wider question, or next paragraph.
- **WHW**: What – How – Why: designed to examine the process of thinking and explain what is happening, how it works, and why it's important.

For long-answer questions, it's interesting to show students how they can structure essays and identify the key components of a long answer. While modelling and live worked examples can be great, often students will struggle to write from a blank page. Structure strips – a pre-prepared strip of paper that students can stick next to their essay in a book, or on a page – enable them to see the big ideas. You can also colour-code answers so students can develop the metacognitive skills of identifying which 'bits' of the answer they have done where, and 'checking their thinking' – building further on that disciplinary thinking.

As we move towards A-level, students can sometimes find the lack of a universally applicable scaffold to be quite frustrating. The classic 'for – against – conclusion' approach that scored well in a long-answer question from GCSE does not translate clearly to an A-level essay. There are a few ways of stimulating that development, and some scaffolds that can be used as part of your teaching conversation at A-level. If it's a binary 'this or that' prompt, a 'washing line' debate can be helpful. You define the two ends of the line as the extremes, and ask students to identify where they think they want to put the peg. In the middle? 50/50? 60/40? 70/30? They can then use the sides of the line to annotate and identify the key points they want to make in support of one side (or the counter arguments to the other).

For questions where there are more than two perspectives, consider scaffolding using a 'pie chart'. Provide (or quickly sketch) a circle, and ask students to fill up the pie chart with different factors – most important first. As before, the students can fill up (or annotate around) the pie chart with the key factors that they want to use in their paragraphs to explain and justify those factors as important. The critical follow-up conversation is 'explain why you put the lines where you did '. This requires students to evaluate why they ranked one thing first, or allocated this proportion of the pie to one factor rather than another. Their judgements and evidence for this conversation are exactly the kind of critical discussion that pushes them towards those highest marks; and this approach can replace essay planning as a concept of bullet point lists or paragraphs – students can quickly assign the lines, and use in exam conditions if they want to do so.

Critical reflection

There is a tension between the concepts of scaffolding for the pure learning of geography, and the translation of that geography in to 'good exam outcomes', or judgements about quality of written communication. On a pragmatic level, both elements need to be considered in an examined course, and we would arguably not be doing our jobs as teachers if we focused only on geography to the exclusion of good results. It is for individuals to decide where scaffolds are deployed, and the extent to which they focus on exam approaches or great learning. They are often most enjoyable to use at KS3 for this reason – the lack of perceived 'exam skills' can be freeing for the approaches we want to take in our classrooms.

Scaffolding is, and should be, much more than just helping a weaker student access information. Used effectively, it can be a training ground for advanced geographical skills and thinking, and ultimately for progression towards disciplinary thinking in the subject! As ever, the key is to plan really effectively – considering your purpose, your context, and the longer arc of the learning sequence beyond the lesson.

Spending time in the geography

One of the biggest weaknesses of the application of the gradual release model is the way in which people believe that, somehow, they can move directly from learning to an exam-type question without spending any time consolidating or practising the geography before. It's very common to see people teach a concept, move to a brief check for understanding, and then immediately hand over to something that looks like a GCSE-style exam question. With the pressures of curriculum, at KS4 in particular, this can sometimes be an understandable response to lesson demands. But – as Roberts (2023) suggests – for good geography, it's important to spend time using the information to create new meaning or learn new techniques.

Fiorella & Mayer's work on generative learning (2015) outlined the core principles of this technique. By selecting and organising information, and 'doing something' with the information – assembling it in to a diagram, for example – the learner is actively engaged in recall, selection and a range of cognitive processes.

> ### Reading recommendation
>
> Mark & Zoe Enser's *Fiorella & Mayer's Generative Learning In Action* (2020) is a really interesting summary of Fiorella & Mayer's eight key principles. They look at how we can develop activities and meaningful student learning through deliberate choice of techniques. As you'd expect, there's a balanced consideration of application and limitations for the strategies in a school context.
>
> You may also be interested to read Alistair Hamill's work on generative learning through diagrams and field sketches made using GIS (Hamill, 2021a).

How do we know how it's going?

Over the course of a sequence of learning, you'll want to take the students on a journey. Where are you currently? How do you know they're with you? How can you move them on? Thinking about that end point, how do you work back through key moments and waypoints? What's the core knowledge they need? Do you introduce hinge questions there? What hinterland would you want to explore? Do you embed and extend through Socratic questioning for everyone? How will you stretch the students' understanding? Thinking of the learning like a journey, or a geographical story, might help you to put questioning in like punctuation, and phrase the stages of work. The purpose and the geography should be at the heart of your planning – and should drive the questions that you want to ask during any particular moment.

At each point when you've introduced a chunk of new material, you'll want to check for understanding. It's important to acknowledge that using such checks – formative assessment – is an intrinsic part of Mode A teaching.

This is partly about cognitive load, and partly about ensuring that your class are with you and you haven't lost anyone. We are checking for interim understanding – the students can only show you what they've learned in the little step you've just taken – rather than a synoptic understanding of the whole process, or a check of prior learning.

When it comes to interim checks like this during explanations, you might want to think about:

- **Prior learning:** Can the students show how their previous knowledge connects to what you've just explained?
- **Specialist vocabulary:** Can the students define or explain words that you've introduced as part of the vocabulary in this explanation? Can they say them? Can they spell them? Do they know where they fit on a diagram or in an explanation?
- **Specialist concepts:** Can the students define and explain key concepts that underpin the explanation?
- **Diagram drawing:** This is often a procedural check, and helpful to do before their practice begins. You can diagnose individual lines and components of the drawing and check the understanding at the same time!

At the earlier stages of your career, these kinds of questions *need* to be planned in advance. Some people annotate lesson plans (or their resource) with the questions they intend to ask, while others do that over a longer term (e.g., over a whole medium-term plan). As you develop your expertise, you'll have a mental plan of how these questions automatically connect – and the schema will develop so you'll always pause *here* and ask that *there*. If you observe skilled experts, they might not even realise that they're doing certain types of questioning – it's become automatic!

One of the ways to move students' understanding on is through Socratic questions. These are designed to challenge the students' existing knowledge and can be helpful to develop complexity and deeper understanding starting with simple answers. In *Making every lesson count*, Allison & Tharby (2015) identify six types of Socratic question:

- Classify thinking (What do you know about ...? What kind of problem is that? What kind of category does that fall in to?).
- Probe assumptions (What does that depend on? What needs to happen to get that result? What would change your answer?).
- Demand evidence (Give me an example. What evidence have we got for that? Where might we see this taking place?).
- Consider alternative viewpoints (Who might disagree? How might residents feel about that? What about people whose homes aren't protected by the flood defence scheme?).
- Explore the implications (So what? But what happens if the sea level rises? Who will be worst impacted?).
- Question the premise of the question (Why does this matter? Do we need to think about this?).

These types of questions form part of a dialogue in a classroom where discussion, debate, and questioning all form a critical part of the learning process. You might find this more challenging with a class of 30 than with a small A-level set, but it can be worth exploring – particularly if paired with think–pair–share activities where students discuss with each other, rather than all the class feeding back at the same time! Knowing how to skilfully use Socratic questions is a key technique in managing debate and evaluative discussions, but it's important that questions are deliberate, thoughtful, and geographical.

Like the check for understanding, these questions are best prepared as part of your planning – they might occur spontaneously but will be much better in the flow of the lesson if you can consider them beforehand. As part of your planning, you can think about:

- What geographical aspects and clarity of understanding do you want to ask about?
- Who are you going to ask? Do you have specific learning needs to consider?
- What stretching questions can you ask the student who asked a brilliant question last lesson?
- How can you hear from a student who's normally a bit quieter in your lesson?

Then you might want to think about some of the more logistical elements that need to be considered to keep the flow of your lesson! For example:

- You might script them, to say aloud. Where does your script live? Lesson plan? Notes of the slide deck?
- You might prepare a slide so you can use them as a 'do now'. You might have questions as part of your lesson resources, or reminders to self about what and how you'll ask certain things.
- You might even print a quiz – or prepare an interactive activity using self-marking software of some kind.

But good question planning should be right at the heart of your lesson planning – and it starts with detailed core geographical knowledge. Some of those key questions will be strongly linked to threshold concepts to check the students are with us in their understanding, and to maximise their thinking ratio.

> **Reading recommendation**
>
> For a greater understanding of Mode A teaching and more discussion of some of the techniques here, I recommend Mark Enser's book *Making every geography lesson count* (2019). There are clear and structured examples of challenge, expert explanations, checks for understanding and feedback approaches, and it's an excellent guide for teachers, particularly in the early stages of their career.

Mode A teaching and thinking is probably going to be the most common aspect of your classroom practice. Getting a structured and thoughtful plan, grounded in disciplinary thinking and expert subject knowledge is the biggest asset in delivering it well, and ensuring students are learning great geography, skills and knowledge of places and examples.

But alongside that, we want to be able to inspire a sense of curiosity, awe and wonder, and to have the flexibility to take less direct instructional approaches to teaching, learning and experiencing geography in a disciplinary way. That's where our Mode B lessons come in …

CHAPTER 8
HOW DO WE INSPIRE AWE AND WONDER IN THE GEOGRAPHY CLASSROOM?

Geography has lots of exciting opportunities to inspire awe and wonder in students, and you may find that Mode B teaching can be more common than the original 80/20 suggestion from Sherrington (2017). Given the practical and timetable realities of many school contexts, there may be many more opportunities to go for this kind of lesson than we might be able to take.

While there are some 'standalone' Mode B activities and approaches, often the best way to really bring out the best in our students is to embed them into a curriculum that has built up their knowledge and understanding first. When they have done a sequence of learning, and are confident on the topic, a Mode B lesson can be an ideal way to apply and explore that knowledge further. Confident curriculum sequencing, and understanding what knowledge, concepts, vocabulary or skills are required to get the best out of an individual activity, remains at the heart of what makes great geography.

Roberts (2023) recommends several excellent practices, many of which fall under the category of Mode B lesson or unit-of-work approaches.

Reading recommendation

Margaret Roberts is synonymous with enquiry approaches to geography, and published several *Teaching Geography* articles and papers before the first edition of *Geography through enquiry* in 2003. The revised 2023 edition gives insight into a disciplinary approach and the benefits of enquiry in the classroom, together with case studies, updated discussions and suggestions which give inspiration and ideas for excellent geography lessons. This book is recommended for teachers and leaders at all stages of their career and can be used as inspiration for curriculum design as well as lesson planning and activities.

Decision-making exercises

Decision-making exercises are an excellent example of a Mode B lesson which is deeply embedded into the disciplinary thinking of geography. After spending time learning about the context, challenge or process of a place or case study problem, students are given realistic information about solutions, stakeholders and parameters, and asked to make and justify their decisions. They may write this up as an individual project or response, or produce a report or presentation, or discuss their findings as a group activity.

To get the best out of decision-making exercises, it's helpful to think about:

- **Where does it fit within the curriculum sequence?** To get the most geographically representative approach, it's best for students to have knowledge and understanding to work from. It's quite common to see a decision-making exercise as the summative activity of a medium-term plan or an enquiry-framed scheme of learning – it is the space in the curriculum where students get to apply their learning to a new context.

- **What are the structures and scaffolds required to support the best geography rather than assessing a proxy of learning?** As you consider your decision-making exercise activity, it's important to think about how we can judge the geographical outcomes and quality of decisions or evaluation, rather than proxies like the quality of written communication, or presentation style and quality. Being clear about how 'a good decision' is made, and focusing on the dimensions of stakeholder engagement or conceptual frameworks (environmental impact versus economic impact) helps students to spend more time thinking about the quality of their geography than the formatting of their response!

- **How do you ensure that the outcomes are appropriate for the geographical learning?** For many areas of the curriculum, this might not be relevant, but it is particularly important to think about what students are taking away when they are conducting this in the context of examined assessments. If you do a decision-making exercise about a real case study, there is a risk that students learn or take away their own decisions, rather than 'what really happened'. This comes with assessment and outcome risks that you may not want to take: it can often feel safer to do decision-making on non-assessed portions of a KS4/5 curriculum (e.g. in association with fieldwork or enquiry), or to explore case studies at KS3.

Decision-making exercises are an incredible opportunity for students to 'think like a geographer' and have huge potential for direct links in to careers and related elements of our curriculum spaces too. In **case study 8.1, Kelly Daish** describes how she has implemented decision-making into her curriculum at The Vyne School.

Debates and role-playing activities

Similarly, debates and role-playing activities (e.g., hot seating) can offer an in-depth look at stakeholder perceptions of an issue. There may be more links to these kinds of activities for wicked problems, or issues which do not have a clear and obvious solution – and hence the value is in deepening student understanding of how and why people feel the way they do about issues, rather than making a decision.

Just like the decision-making exercises, they are often best used in the latter stages of a scheme of work, with students given informed or research-driven approaches to take on particular roles or views. As well as this curriculum mindset, it's worth thinking about:

- How you set up and allocate the roles within the class. There will be some students who will relish 'taking on a character' from an acting or performative perspective, and there will be others who will enjoy the depth of research or approach to understanding a stakeholder view. There will be plenty who don't want to – or find it harder – to access either of those roles.
- How many roles and approaches you create within the classroom space, and how you can equitably share those around. If there are 5–8 individual stakeholders, how does that work for a class of 30+ students? This might be simpler if there are organisations, countries or larger groups that can be represented by a small group of students – but it's worth thinking about how you balance out the roles, and how you deliberately choose to assign them.
- How do you facilitate the activity in terms of behaviours and relationships? These kinds of debates or discussion activities require a strong understanding of the specifics of your classroom culture and context, and tend to be most successful later in the year when you have established strong relationships with your students!

One of the other key challenges is often thinking about how this translates to individual outcomes or learning, and how (if) you know. It can be tempting to hold a whole-class debate, or a hot seat activity, and then ask students to write an essay/individual response to check for understanding. How do you ensure that there's a relationship between what you've asked them to do originally (discuss, debate, perhaps even research) and the follow-up assessment or judgement on a completely different skill set or activity? You may choose not to set an assessed piece of work afterwards, but you then need to reflect on how confident you can then be about everyone's participation or learning, and the extent to which your wider setting would be confident with that outcome!

Games, simulations, and data

Online platforms and tools offer live modelling or experimental opportunities for students to actively apply learning or test hypotheses in a realistically generated environment. Some of them have more game-like interfaces – where students follow their own paths, or generate actions – and these are often better suited to individual activities or out-of-the-classroom work than a lesson. Some offer opportunities for data visualisation and analysis (e.g., the online census data, live electricity or carbon-tracking websites, Gapminder's tool sets and supporting data packages, or displays of global environmental variables such as https://earth.nullschool.net/) and these are likely to work best with teacher 'from the front' instruction, or as part of a skill development activity where there are specific research or plotting requirements.

In between are those where there is scope for students to be engaged as a whole class in an activity that tests understanding or application of knowledge in lessons. This might be carbon footprint calculators, or sites linked to climate scenarios, such as in the En-ROADS simulator described **in Extras 8.1.**

When you're using tools and simulators like this, it's important to consider the classroom and curriculum context (Burger et al., 2023). The potential for overlap with individual assessments of learning is a little stronger, but the considerations for curriculum, behaviour and relationship development are equally valid things to consider.

Use of GIS and related tools

We should ideally be teaching GIS as a regular and standard part of our Mode A lessons, and it should ideally be so integrated into our work that it becomes part of our daily way of working. For many classroom teachers, it *can* be part of Mode A explanations as a 'teaching from the front', and there are number of excellent practitioners who regularly demonstrate 'how I used GIS today' in lesson content, teacher-led activities and to add geographical and place-based context to lessons in a meaningful and instruction-led way.

However, the relatively low likelihood of regular access to ICT resources, or the professional development of staff in procedural knowledge and confidence, means that we are still collectively working towards a position where GIS can be embedded within our curriculum as a Mode A approach for our students to use as a way of working.

I think we would like to work towards a position where GIS became more of an everyday experience for our students consistently across all classrooms, but there's still a long way to go from a resource, curriculum and development perspective. Some considerations are discussed in **Extras 8.2** but the principles of a curricular approach to mapping and GIS will be explored further in the next chapter.

Research and project-based learning

It's important to acknowledge that project-based learning and inquiry-led student research is disciplinarily distinct from the principles of geographical enquiry we have described earlier (Roberts, 2023). Although you may overlap them and blend one into another, they are not the same by default.

There is also a notable difference between a directed 'virtual fieldwork' style activity, where we are teaching and leading research using tools in lieu of being able to investigate an issue in the real world, and a research or inquiry project which is less directive.

Encouraging students to take on a sustained project (over multiple lessons, or in groups) is different from looking up resources over a short term, or using data within a single lesson, or a flipped learning approach. It takes a substantially different mindset to think about how to design, plan and facilitate research over multiple lessons that is effective, geographically sound, and allows for confident assessment of learning for all (Habib, 2023). In many cases, we need to think about:

- What are we investigating as a project? Why is it relevant for the curriculum or topic in question?

- What are the trade-offs in having students find their own information (e.g., Rackley, 2018), case study or focus, rather than a whole-class question and more standardised approach?
- How are we setting up the project in terms of individuals and groups? If individual, we need to think about scaffolds, support and ensuring all learners have access to high-quality outcomes; if we are thinking about groups, how do we ensure that all students are participating and getting the best learning possible?
- How can we scaffold and direct the work enough to ensure that progress and engagement is effective, without taking away the 'independence' of the project?

There is no question that independent investigation is a vital skill to acquire, and it's even a core disciplinary approach that is assessed through the NEA at A-level. I'm a huge fan of project qualifications, like the Extended Project Qualification (EPQ), too. But in both cases, the rigorous scaffolding and structure is what enables those outcomes and successes to be possible, and it takes a huge amount of time, effort and skill on the part of the facilitators and project leaders.

Student-led research in geography lessons can be a hugely powerful tool, and a really positive experience in developing skills and confidence in their own interpretation of the world – but it does often take significantly more teacher effort and skill than first appears.

Critical reflection

A cautionary note on the cost–benefit of Mode B lessons

There are a number of options for Mode B lessons, and a series of activities and tasks that can be potentially included in that group, or things that appear to be 'awe and wonder' lessons. Some of them, though, move towards activities that might be better suited to extracurricular settings. For example, over the course of my teaching career, I've:

- Used cakes or food items to make and model geographic features or erosion. At some stage, I even ran a 'cake tectonics' competition which persisted mostly because I really liked the pun in the title.
- Spent two to four lessons using cameras, plasticine and modelling to generate stop-motion animation explanations for landform development (e.g., cave, arch and stack formation).

- Asked students to build 'an example of informal housing' using recycled materials as a homework project.
- Spent four lessons researching, scripting and filming 'adverts' to persuade people of a particular viewpoint on a contested issue topic.

There's no question that the thought and intention as we planned the curriculum was positive, and lots of the students enjoyed them at the time, too. I'm less confident that the key geographical points of the content would have been remembered over time and, on reflection, I don't know if they were worth the lesson (and homework, research and between-lesson) time and resources that were involved.

It can be tempting to do some interesting things in the name of a Mode B-style lesson, but it's vital that you make a deliberate and mindful decision based on a cost–benefit analysis of what and how you're teaching. There are things that you may judge to be worthwhile, and it's important that you are able to reflect on their value *to geography*, your students and your context on an individual and specific basis.

CHAPTER 9
HOW DO WE TEACH GEOGRAPHICAL SKILLS IN THE CLASSROOM?

No matter what your specification or context, the process of teaching and learning about geography involves a huge range of implicit knowledge and skills that are needed in order to access our content. You can't just teach subject knowledge in isolation – accessing our subject means that students need to be able to 'do' a lot of things, too. Often, they are linked to exam specifications, and so we need to have them by the end of KS4.

In addition to the range of skills, students should be able to:

- identify questions and sequences of enquiry
- write descriptively, analytically and critically
- communicate their ideas effectively and develop an extended written argument
- draw well-evidenced and informed conclusions about geographical questions and issues.

This requires a geographical approach to literacy and communication skills, so these need to be taught and embedded throughout the curriculum. It's clear that, to be able to be a good geographer, you have to balance knowing a breadth of content, with being able to do a wide range of different things.

How do I develop geographical literacy?

Whole-school literacy strategies are best understood in the context of your school. What we're going to focus on here is the concepts associated with 'disciplinary literacy' – the specific set of vocabulary, reading and writing skills associated with our subject (Chandler, 2022).

There are two key conceptual components of literacy that are important for us to think about (Bishop & Preece, 2024).

- **At the lesson scale**, how do we do individual activities that develop a specific skill?

- **At the curriculum scale,** how do we make progress through time to build fluency? How do we make this increasingly automatic – and how do we use our understanding of cognitive science principles to help? How do we make this increasingly strategic – and use some of the curriculum planning principles to embed this development in our medium- and long-term planning?

Why do we need to develop vocabulary?

Most specifications provide a subject-specific vocabulary list, which is useful to discuss in your planning and with your department. One of the biggest challenges of geography at GCSE for teachers and students alike is the sheer volume of content providing cognitive overwhelm.

There are several techniques that can be used to help you teach new vocabulary. One of the most popular and effective is the Frayer model, based on a template developed to help organise understanding of a new term or complex vocabulary choice. Students are asked to co-construct a grid of four key thoughts about a piece of vocabulary to clarify what it is, the key features, and examples and non-examples of use (see Figure 6).

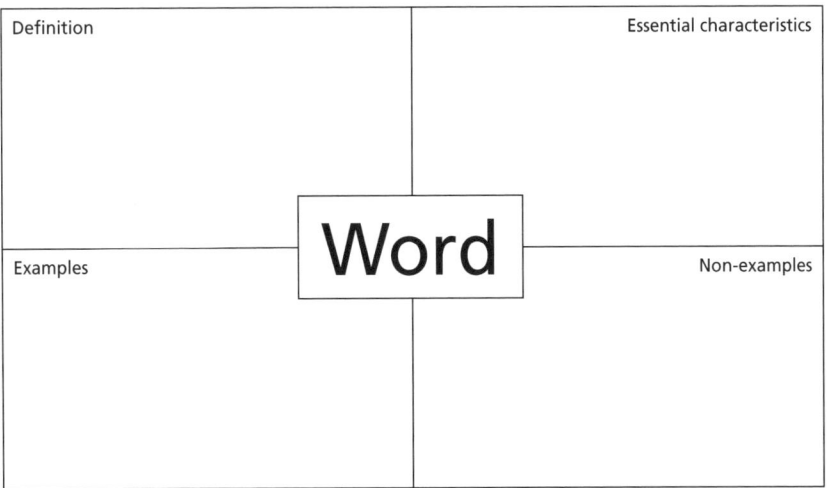

▲ Figure 6: An example of a Frayer model grid

While this is an excellent pedagogical principle, there is no question that there is a significant cost in terms of lesson time and content. You could use all of your learning hours teaching the expected vocabulary for the GCSE course – and that's without any understanding of theories, processes, or case studies and context. For learners with any additional challenges – whether that's in terms of neurodiversity, additional learning needs, or having English as an additional language – this is a huge structural obstacle to accessing great geography.

One solution is to try a 'flipped learning' approach to vocabulary: setting students vocabulary to learn as a structured homework. Facer (2016) reflects on how the Michaela Community School took this approach using flashcards and vocabulary books. Technology can help you systematise this. Students can access flashcards and quizzes from different devices in multiple formats, and have access to standardised vocabulary lists which provide a consistent (and exam-specification) appropriate definition. Some platforms allow you to set up classes and structures which dovetail with your own learning platforms, or set and monitor students' progress directly.

It's important to have a longer-term discussion and vision in mind for these activities. They need to be carefully thought out, considered and embedded over a curriculum, as a deliberate strategy (Bishop & Preece, 2024). If you reflect on the vocabulary listed in your GCSE specification, you can consider how you might sort the terms into one of three categories:

- Words you'd expect a KS3 student in your school context to know or understand as part of their regular curriculum.
- Words you'd expect a KS3 student in your school context to have learned in their geography lessons prior to starting their GCSE course.
- Words that you'd anticipate deliberately having to teach a KS4 student that you can group them together to provide some kind of cohesive vocabulary unit for each topic.

It's likely that a substantial proportion of the list in your specification is actually taught and embedded from KS3 curriculum thinking, freeing you up to focus on the terminology new to KS4, or to explore misconceptions or known issues for your community and context. This is why it's so vital to have a joined-up approach to your curriculum intent and implementation.

We should also recognise the role that wider cultural capital and our colleagues might be able to play in supporting the development of our students' vocabulary. Working together with other departments and subjects can be a powerful way to build curriculum coherence, and help us understand what our students are seeing in different places. It can also be critical in highlighting misconceptions: sometimes we see that words have different meaning in other subjects, and it's helpful to be able to plan to avoid these. As ever, teaching is a team sport – keep asking how you can make use of your colleagues, other departments and literacy leads to get the best outcomes for your students.

Developing reading skills

The systematic and strategic development of literacy in our students is intrinsically linked to a question about what we're asking them to read. Myatt (2016) describes the use of deliberately challenging texts to explore and enrich students' disciplinary and curriculum experiences. In geography, we have a vast range of books that we can explore through our curriculum (e.g., Stockings, 2023a; 2023b).

While there's a discussion about the most effective way to do whole-class reading (EEF, 2021) and the time it would take in geography, it's clear that it needs to be carefully planned. Just like any other element of your lesson planning, you need to consider your objectives and then set out the way that you're going to maximise student outcomes. Graves & Graves (2003) describe this as 'scaffolded reading', and set out the steps as follows:

- Pre-reading: Before you begin reading, you need to give the students a link and set them up for success: for example, by setting the context or focus for reading, recapping prior knowledge, or identifying specific vocabulary that will be needed.
- During reading: How do you manage the reading process and discussions? You might have ways of clarifying concepts, ideas and vocabulary, or pointing out key elements.
- Post reading: Once the text engagement is concluded, students will need to translate that in to learning outcomes and make it meaningful for them. This might include discussions, writing, or activities designed to help students clarify or apply their thinking.

It's important that you think carefully about the reading – both in terms of the deliberate practice and how to make it accessible and purposeful, but also in terms of the choice of what you're asking your students to read. We want to make sure that the texts are directly related to what we want to achieve, and that they give students great geography understanding and disciplinary thinking. We also want to make sure that we have a wide representation of texts that reflect different perspectives on the world.

When you think about what texts and sources you are selecting to include (Stockings, 2023; 2023b), you might want to think about:

- What geographical purpose is the text is serving?
- What perspectives and views of the world does it show?
- What authors and representation are you including? Are you showing a range of places, gender equalities or social inequalities? How do those weave through the curriculum experience?

Supporting adaptive pedagogies of reading and literacy

As well as considering how we aim for challenging and stretching reading for all, it's important to acknowledge the particular need to add support for some of our students in particular. As well as the vocabulary challenges identified earlier, studies show that geography is one of the most complex subjects in terms of reading levels required for success, second only to English literature (GL Reports, 2020), and it is therefore vital that we consider ways to adapt our pedagogy and reading levels to suit the needs of a range of students.

As a geography teacher, there are two key challenges that make it difficult to do this well.

- At the time of writing, there is not a huge depth of subject-specific literature or approaches to learn from, although the Bell Foundation (https://www.bell-foundation.org.uk/) offers good subject-specific ideas. However, there are plenty of great resources for EAL or literacy across all subjects.
- The wide breadth of our curriculum, the specifics of case studies and the constructed nature of our subject inevitably mean that you might have to make your own resources and tailor them exactly to your curriculum. This is a significant workload burden on teachers – particularly if you want to embed structural approaches like the Frayer model for your key vocabulary, or create adapted reading experiences for particular students or challenges.

Emily Chandler (2022) developed practical strategies for using a range of texts. She has built on that to show how teachers might consider using ChatGPT and other specific tools to improve student accessibility with less impact on teacher workload (Chandler, 2024). You may want to explore using Diffit (https://web.diffit.me/) and Wordsift (https://wordsift.org/) as tools to scale text up and down for different reading ages, and to simply and powerfully create resources that serve the learners' needs and develop the vocabulary and structures of learning!

We must ensure that all students have access to a rich diet of great geography, which includes incredible reading. We have many opportunities to ask them to read as geographers do, and to explore high-quality texts with our support. In **case study 9.1, Abdurrahman Pérez-McMillan** gives an insight in to how this is being done across the Year 8 curriculum at the Harris Federation.

Having a thoughtful and considered approach to how we embed the fluent reading of challenging texts – and of supporting and scaffolding all students to be able to access them – is a key part of bringing geography alive. It is part of our discipline and our world, and we want to invite our students to join that conversation with confidence. But it's not the only lens we use, and we need to be able to ensure a broad range of skills that accompany literacy, some of which are uniquely geographical.

Cartographic and digital mapping skills

Geographers think about the world in spatial terms. Spatial thinking is a term used to describe the desirable outcome of geographical study: to analyse, interpret and describe 'spatial patterns and organisation of people, places, and environments on Earth' (Ofsted, 2021).

Place, space and locational knowledge is at the heart of geography, and lots of the connections and approaches are focused on:

- Identifying where things are – place and locational knowledge.
- Being able to describe and identify the features of a landscape or place.
- Being able to connect place and other information using maps as a base to locate other knowledge, patterns and trends.

But we can't think spatially as an abstract concept. We need to connect the relationships and ideas we have to the representations of space – and geographers visualise and analyse spatial relationships between objects as a key part of our discipline. Through the use of maps, students are presented with a spatially referenced framework and visual cues. Building on this visualisation, students draw on concepts they have already learned, such as location, distance, direction, shape and pattern.

Taught well, spatial thinking develops a meaningful sense of place and appreciation of the interconnectedness of the subject. We might think of

103

maps, atlases and globes as a bit of a cliché, or a gently stereotyped view of our subject – particularly at school level – but, in reality, they are a vital part of our curriculum.

Cartographic skills relate to the use and interpretation of a variety of maps at different scales. This might be to provide contextual and background information – looking at specific place knowledge, including being able to draw evidence and infer human use, landscape and activity – or as to represent specific patterns or data. Students are likely to need to become familiar with the use, recognition and interpretation of:

- Atlas maps, and a range of 'base maps', at a variety of scales.
- OS maps. It's worth getting hold of an OS map for your school's area and getting comfortable with some of the skills that you need to be able to teach your students!
- Using maps in association with photographs to interpret, infer, analyse and annotate.

We should be embedding mapwork regularly through our curriculum – not just to support long-term exam skill development, but also because it's great geography and the foundation of our discipline. It is, therefore, critical to have a curriculum mindset and to frequently use maps right the way from Year 7 all the way up to GCSE and A-level across multiple topics and lessons rather than as a standalone or one-off experience.

Of course, the modern world works on GIS and we don't all use paper maps exclusively. Teaching with interactive and online software is an important part of developing a sense of place in your lessons. You'll want to consider the use of GIS in your curriculum (see Extras 8.1) whether you're teaching 'from the board' (Hamill, 2020; 2024) or actively embedding their use into your students' activities and lesson plans (particularly around fieldwork and investigations). Your school might have a preferred approach and platforms, and you may have enough regular access to computer rooms to teach some of the geoinformatics skills that characterise the best learning.

Using maps, GIS and geographical skills are skills that, like any other, need to be practised regularly. They should be embedded into our curriculum over the medium- and long-term, and we should revisit our thinking about them on a frequent basis. It's helpful to think about:

- What map resource (physical, digital) do you have in your classroom or department? Does every geography classroom have a world map in it?

- How can you *use* the map on a regular basis? Is it at the front, as a teacher resource, or part of a display that fades in to background? Think about plotting all of your case studies on to a world map (which can reveal a fascinating distribution of your examples), and using it regularly to explore locational knowledge.

- How do you show a range of maps – atlas, base maps, different scales, different projections – to get students used to the concept of maps as a power, or as a constructed space? Can you explore the differences between globes and maps, and integrate that with your topics? Consider including maps as sources, or starter materials, or using them as an introduction to case studies. How often do you show a map as a key part of your Mode A teaching, or lesson content?

- How can you embed this without huge cost (classroom sets of atlases!) or showing material that can age and go out of date quite quickly? Most printed maps and materials are regularly updated and reprinted – but it's rare that schools are able to keep up.

- Think about how you might use GIS to demonstrate learning about a location, or integrate it into fieldwork planning. Google Earth can be an effective introduction to a location in Mode A teaching, or even as a form of summative assessment on a project in Mode B!

- How do you ensure that the focus is on the geographical knowledge, not the procedural? Often, where we have aspects of a skill that we rarely use, the majority of the cognitive load and thinking is 'How do I do this? What step is next? What tool am I using?' rather than 'What is this telling me? What is the relationship I'm seeing?' or other geographical questions.

Often, unless you are able to embed cartographic skills into your lessons frequently, you may need to deliberately create reminder and refresher starter activities to use before the core geographical task. It's also important to think about how you regularly brush up on your own skills so that you are confident with directing attention to the geography, or able to anticipate needs and misconceptions from students.

Numerical & statistical skills

Critical reflection
A note on 'maths anxiety'

Some people have a different emotional response to the use of numerical and statistical skills. Teachers and students alike often have a more personal and visceral response to 'maths' than other skills geography, and it's important to acknowledge that.

You may have experienced or be aware of it yourself: you might have preferred human or physical geography because you have your own perspectives and experiences of qualitative or quantitative analysis. That may shape how you embed, or teach the quantitative elements described here. It's important for you to be able to step outside that perspective and objectively explore how the mathematics might work or be necessary for your curriculum and your students.

The range of quantitative skills used in geography is quite diverse (see Table 13). While some are directly related to fieldwork and enquiry, others might be used as source materials for lessons, learning or Mode A teaching on a regular basis. As we move towards more scientific topics, the 'quantitative literacy' required to make sense of probabilities, estimates or likelihoods becomes increasingly important. RMetS runs online courses exploring mathematics for understanding climate change, demonstrating the critical relevance of these skills in certain topics.

▼ Table 13: Examples of numerical and statistical skills expected in geography

Numerical skills to:	• demonstrate an understanding of number, area and scales, and the quantitative relationships between units • design fieldwork data collection sheets and collect data with an understanding of accuracy, sample size and procedures, control groups and reliability • understand and correctly use proportion and ratio, magnitude and frequency.

Statistical skills to:	• draw informed conclusions from numerical data
	• use appropriate measures of central tendency, spread and cumulative frequency (median, mean, range, quartiles and inter-quartile range, mode and modal class)
	• calculate percentage increase or decrease and understand the use of percentiles
	• describe relationships in bivariate data: sketch trend lines through scatter plots, draw estimated lines of best fit, make predictions, interpolate and extrapolate trends
	• identify weaknesses in selective statistical presentation of data.
At A-level, many exam boards add additional statistical skills to the list, including:	• measurement, measurement errors, and sampling tests of association and significance tests, such as chi-squared, Spearman's rank, Mann-Whitney U test, and t-test.
	• calculated lines of best fit and correlation on graphical representations.

We should be embedding these skills, and their application to geographical knowledge, in our curriculum where they are helpful and appropriate. It's more likely that we'll do this in higher key stages, but it's possible to have quantitative work on a regular basis in our KS3 curriculum content when using source material, or connected with maps, graphs and spatial representations of data.

However, unlike mapping, there are cross-curricular considerations here. Our colleagues in maths and science will be using lots of the same numerical and statistical skills and, at KS5, there is also likely to be overlap with economics, business or psychology. How can you identify what's happening where, and see it in action? It's helpful to consider:

- What mathematical, numerical and statistical skills and experiences would you anticipate students coming into Year 7 with?
- How and where are numerical and statistical skills taught and revisited in your geography curriculum? Which ones are specifically taught when? (e.g., descriptive statistics in Year 8 population).

- How and where do you use quantitative data as source material to develop case studies or specific knowledge in your teaching of places? What kind of data do you use? How often do you use different types?
- How and where do you combine this with base maps to introduce spatial patterns and trends?
- Where else in your school curriculum are these ideas introduced, taught and revisited? How do you know? Can you observe teaching in any of those departments? Does it help to be able to make explicit links to their curriculum or approaches?

Critical reflection

Although there is reasonable agreement in the geography community on the importance of cartographic skills and numerical skills, there is not necessarily the same agreement about what it means to 'get better' at them and develop through time. Most approaches to skill progression focus on procedural fluency or competence (in other words, taking less effort to achieve the same outcome) or the application of a slightly more complex variation of the skill.

One might conceptually describe progression in 'significance' as moving from descriptive skills (line of best fit) to mathematical skills (correlation coefficient) to statistical (t-test of significance). This would move us towards a more 'scientific' analysis of an outcome, and a more quantitative approach, but it is less obvious if this is 'getting better' at the skill or simply applying a further methodological step.

It is also not clear – or coherently understood – how this relates to progress in *geography* specifically. What *geographical* difference does it make to be able to quantify a significance, rather than to just describe it? There are elements of our work (e.g., IPCC confidence intervals) where that statistical confidence and understanding is a critical component of the geographical understanding, but these are comparatively rare.

There is still plenty of disciplinary thinking and work to do to explore dimensions of progress in areas of our curriculum, and ongoing discussions and debates about how they should sit alongside curriculum models, specifications and assessment frameworks.

Graphical skills

As well as being able to read other people's data, we want our students to be able to show their thinking and geographical findings. That means being able to select and plot data using a range of visual methods and graphs. A list of required graphical skills might include:

- Select and construct appropriate graphs and charts to present data, using appropriate scales – line charts, bar charts, pie charts, pictograms, histograms with equal class intervals, divided bar, scatter graphs, and population pyramids.
- Suggest an appropriate form of graphical representation for data provided.
- Complete a variety of graphs and maps – choropleth, isoline, dot maps, desire lines, proportional symbols, and flow lines.
- Use and understand gradient, contour and value on isoline maps.
- Plot information on graphs when axes and scales are provided.
- Interpret and extract information from different types of maps, graphs, and charts, including population pyramids, choropleth maps, flow-line maps, dispersion graphs.

Our colleagues in maths and science will be doing lots of graphing and plotting – and there might be other subject areas which use this skill set too. However, one of the challenges of a subject like geography in relation to these skills, in particular, is that we are constantly seeking to ensure that our datasets and graphical information is up to date and relevant. Although there are some examples of graphs and data that we might be able to use, or plot, on a regular basis without any hesitation (e.g., distribution of insolation by latitude, or an annual climate graph for a location), it's common for other data to change much more regularly.

Critical reflection

Although cross-curricular working can appear like an ideal solution from a teacher and learner perspective, it can sometimes introduce false hope.

In some science lessons, for example, students are taught different ways of plotting specific graphs, that they then must 'unlearn' in a geography lesson. Students may learn different thresholds for application of statistical tests in mathematics, or use specific vocabulary in slightly different ways. Our approaches to literacy or key frameworks may be slightly different to the way they are integrated in history or English.

As well as looking for areas of alignment, it is good practice to try and identify if there are any potential areas of misconception that can be introduced, or areas where there is divergence of technique that it is useful to know about in advance!

The relationship between skills, fieldwork and geographical enquiry

One of the key aspects to acknowledge in this space is the implicit relationship between the nature and purpose of these skills and the wider disciplinary context that they sit in. Some skills – particularly on exam board specifications – are listed primarily so that they could be legitimately used with data sources as prompts or questions in an examination. For many others, there's an intrinsic link and expectation between the skills that we teach and the processes of fieldwork investigation, or an enquiry cycle, that support the principles of some of our disciplinary learning. This may not be obvious unless your own curriculum principles and thinking are aligned with significant opportunities to do fieldwork, or to develop that through time. You can see the relationship between the practice and enquiry sequence, and many of the skills and understanding elements developed through classroom and fieldwork opportunities, in Table 14.

Although Kitchen (2025: 6) shows that fieldwork is about more than the six stage enquiry, the progression model for fieldwork (Kitchen, 2025: figure 8) shows that development of question, data, analysis and reflection and evaluation skills are critical to ensuring development towards independent geographical enquiry. It may be helpful to think about the progression order for each of the rows in Table 14, to help identify the ways in which you can work from simplest to hardest skills in different domains.

▼ Table 14: Geographical practice in classroom and field (Roberts, 2021; GA 2022: 10).

Geographical practice: enquiry sequence	Elements of practice including enquiry processes, skills and understandings developed in the classroom and in the field
Identifying geographical questions. **Observing, perceiving, identifying.**	Being aware of the geographical questions that underpin geographical knowledge, e.g., What? Where? When? Why? Who? How? What might? What ought? Being aware of and asking questions related to what is being studied. Recognising questions through fieldwork, reading, media images, discussion.
Identifying, gathering and using sources of geographical information. **Defining, extracting, describing.**	Identifying what is needed to pursue enquiries. Searching for and selecting relevant sources of information. Evaluating the credibility and reliability of sources of information. Identifying the influence of values and evaluating accuracy and identifying bias and/or false information. Presenting information in different formats, e.g., in diagrams, tables, graphs. Extracting significant information and describing, classifying and categorising it. Sources of information, including digital sources: e.g., maps, statistics, graphs, photographs, satellite images, film, text (reports, newspapers, poems, fiction, blogs, digital media), works of art, promotional materials, personal geographies.
Analysing and making sense of information. **Analysing, explaining, making connections.**	Relating sources and data to everyday knowledge, to what is known geographically, and to theories and models. Using statistical techniques to analyse quantitative data. Comparing, contrasting and interpreting qualitative material. Identifying relationships, impacts and trends. Analysing and clarifying values.

Geographical practice: enquiry sequence	Elements of practice including enquiry processes, skills and understandings developed in the classroom and in the field
Predicting, thinking creatively, problem-solving. **Envisaging, speculating, applying.**	Making suggestions about future trends and impacts, using data in different ways. Thinking creatively about issues and viewpoints. Designing alternative models and futures. Making decisions and suggesting solutions.
Reaching conclusions. **Summarising, drawing together, presenting.**	Giving reasoned explanations or interpretations. Relating findings and fieldwork experiences to geographical knowledge and theories, highlighting concepts. Weighing up alternatives. Formulating, qualifying and justifying generalisations. Presenting findings and drawing related conclusions.
Reflecting on what has been learned. **Evaluating, responding.**	Evaluating critically the credibility and reliability of sources of information, secondary data used, methods of analysis and interpretation, conclusions reached. Reflecting on further avenues of enquiry and more desk-based research or fieldwork. Clarifying one's own values and moral/ethical stance. Recognising possible courses of action for others and for oneself.

As we described in the critical reflection earlier, it makes sense to acknowledge that this can be the implicit driver of progression models, too. The enquiry strand from the 2020 GA progression model (Figure 3) shows a more sequential development of skills than some of the earlier considerations might indicate. The development of independence in enquiry planning, selection and methodology makes sense in this disciplinary context but, perhaps, is not always obvious in the classroom setting.

Several geographers and curriculum leaders have explicitly written and talked about a deliberately planned 'skills curriculum' that runs through (or is interwoven with) their geography curriculum. If you are thinking about how to identify and develop such a strand, whether for literacy, oracy or the skills linked to fieldwork and enquiry explored in this section, it is worth considering:

- What is the cost–benefit of doing so? It may be easier to start by identifying the components of what you have, where you currently teach, and then looking to 'fill in the gaps'.
- How does it align with your wider philosophies around knowledge, content and geographical principles? If you have lots of fieldwork and opportunities to embed and practice, the strand might be aligned differently than in a more classroom-dominated curriculum.
- What are the opportunities, skills and resources (e.g., ICT, financial, physical) of your team and context? If you have lots of money to spend on atlases, have regular access to IT classrooms, or students with personal devices, and have lots of software downloaded on to machines, it's a different conversation than other schools for whom resourcing is more challenging. How confident are your staff team in their own skills and practice? (Many people are less comfortable with statistics than mapping, for instance!)
- How does your skills curriculum fit with wider school or educational landscapes? At the time of writing, the Oracy Commission had just published their final report (OEC, 2024), and it is likely that we will see a focus on that in schools in the next few years. What are your school priorities, and how do these link in?

There is no question that teaching great geography requires thoughtful consideration of what it means to plan for, and make progress in, the subject. This is just as true for the skills – or philosophical approach to enquiry or fieldwork – that underpins that progression model as it is for the knowledge, content and synoptic thinking that we seek to develop. Let's look at how we plan and assess that progress in the next chapter.

CHAPTER 10
HOW DO WE ASSESS PROGRESS IN THE GEOGRAPHY CURRICULUM?

In chapter 7, we looked at the idea of formative assessment, that which takes place 'in the moment' in the classroom. Here, the focus will shift to look at some of the models and thinking behind planning for progression in geography in a more structured and summative way. You'll notice a lot of deliberate conceptual overlap with the curriculum work from earlier chapters.

The challenge of progression in geography assessment

Assessment should be an integrated part of your planning – both for individual lessons, and for whole units across the curriculum. Opportunities for assessment thoughtfully integrated into lessons reflect a subtle shift in emphasis towards thinking about what students are to learn (rather than simply what activities they are to do). A significant number of the components of curriculum planning are also about skill progression and 'doing geography' rather than 'knowing geography'.

However, there are several proxies for development that may be more about skills than geographical progression. A high-performing student will be better at geography, but also have good essay writing skills to express their ideas fluently. We need to be careful that we know what we are attributing progression to, and that we are aware of the development of the wider reading, writing and data literacy that makes for the appearance of an excellent geographer.

But the non-linear nature of geography means that we've got a challenge in terms of planning those assessments and progress points. Some students will find the numerical skills hard; others will love them but find essay writing difficult. Some students will struggle with map-reading, but love source questions and photographic interpretation.

There is also a challenge with the synoptic nature of our subject, summed up in the phrase 'thinking like a geographer'. You'll see this used in several places – it even used to be on the exam specification as a characteristic of A* at A-level. The idea is to develop 'synoptic' thinking

– the ability to see connections between different places and ideas, and to evaluate and judge them against to each other. This is the heart of our discipline – the connection between human and physical process, places and environments.

For teachers and students alike, the biggest difficulties with 'thinking like a geographer' are that it's hard to define and it's not something you can do straight away. Students can't make connections between different parts of an idea until they've done lots of the parts. You can't teach them to make connections between different themes, topics or places until they've studied a range.

Therefore, it's important to think carefully about how to sequence learning and assessment so that our students are building up to more complex ideas. You'll often see evaluative questions and decision-making exercises used at the end of a unit or scheme of work. This is not just because they're interesting ways to assess, but also because students simply won't be able to access them at the start when their knowledge is much tighter and less broad.

What's the difference between feedback and assessment in geography?

Giving feedback in your classroom – or written diagnostic feedback in student books or on their work – can be hugely powerful. It's important that you build a culture where feedback means just as much thinking for the student as the teacher, and there are several strategies which exist to support that development (e.g., directed improvement and response/reflection time). The feedback then stays true to the original principles: your guidance helps a student to get a better understanding of how to make progress in the targeted area of geography.

What's the nature of summative assessment?

To assess learning effectively in terms of progression through the curriculum, you need to consider your learning activities and summative assessment in terms of their intrinsic value to geography. Table 15 gives examples of how we might consider some components.

▼ Table 15: Considerations for designing assessment in geography

Purpose and clarity	What are you trying to achieve with this activity or assessment?
	Begin with the end in mind here, too.
Geographical versus procedural knowledge	What is the geography you are trying to assess?
	You want to have targeted this, rather than testing how well a graph can be drawn, or how well something is written. It's harder than you think!
Accuracy	How precise do you need the knowledge to be?
	How do you ensure you apply that to a written assessment, or a learning activity?
Reliability	How do you ensure that learning is happening consistently over time?
	You might need to think about cognitive science principles of retrieval and practice.
Breadth of content	How do you ensure that you cover the wide range of ideas from a topic or a unit? How do you select which ones to cover, and how do you know that you've covered all of them over time?
	For example, have you assessed all the different landforms from a rivers or coast unit? All the different types of urban environment?
Depth of content	How do you know that you've covered the content to the right depth, across all the different topics?
Skills development and progression	How are you assessing the development of skills, or testing the mastery of a particular skill?
	Do you want students to get great at using OS maps as sources? Do you want them to practice population pyramid interpretation? Then design them in!
Extent to which you model examination-style questions (or command words)	Some teachers like to consciously reflect the language of their examination specification through their KS3 assessments. Other activities and assessments (e.g., a decision-making exercise) are completely separated from exam-style activities. You might want a poster, or a video, or a completely different way of assessing an outcome!

Timing and accessibility needs:	How do you ensure that there's enough time to do the assessment justice? You will want to think about students who may require extra time, or additional adjustments (e.g., a laptop, larger text or different coloured paper).
Marking considerations	It's often the last thing a teacher thinks about, but assessments shouldn't be workload killers for them. If you can use technology (online multiple-choice questions, for example) to reduce your workload without compromising the geography, that's great. Think about peer assessment, too, and whole-class feedback techniques.

So, to support students developing towards their summative assessment points, we need to assess our students':

- knowledge of the content
- knowledge of vocabulary and terminology
- knowledge of case studies
- skills in numeracy, graphicacy and data response
- fieldwork knowledge
- principles of evaluation and decision-making
- ability to write fluently
- exam skills, including understanding the paper structure and how to make good decisions
- confidence in performing under pressure and against the clock.

This means we need to deliberately plan our assessments (formative, summative and formal), to progressively build up their confidence, as well as our own judgements and confidence in how we can best support them at each stage!

There is a philosophical debate about the extent to which you should mimic examination-style assessments lower down in the school. Some people believe that it provides a helpful 'stepping stone' towards GCSE progress, while others believe that it can lead to unhelpful comparisons, or false understanding of what and how a GCSE grade can be achieved

How do we approach summative assessment in the curriculum?

While the wider principles of curriculum planning and principles of assessment are often high-level conversations that may involve only a small number of people in a school, the operational elements of summative assessment often have an impact on a wider range of teachers. The structures and nature of data drops, reporting cycles and wider communication can be significant drivers of workload, calendars and the rhythm of a term.

Once the school calendar has been decided, it's down to the individual geography department to consider:

- The validity and reliability of assessment and marking.
- The breadth of assessment – how to cover skills, data and content. Will students have the opportunity to do multiple different types of paper across both years of the exam specification, or do they only do some in the latter part of the course, for example? How does that fit with the curriculum and taught content?
- 'Exam skill' development, and the students' exposure to 'exam conditions '. To learn how to avoid rubric errors, students must see full papers so they can learn and practice choices and timings. If students have additional needs, extra time, or access to laptops or scribes, then they need to regularly practice with them. Some schools will hold examinations in classrooms in some years, while others will hold 'mock exams' in the room where the regular exams will take place.
- How to support students (and parents, if appropriate) to learn to revise and prepare properly. What resources and teaching do you provide in that space?

Once the curriculum intent and approach has been established, the marking and tracking of student outcomes is a key driver of workload for teachers. Feedback and assessment are about being deliberate and intentional. You can only close gaps when you know they exist, and you can only improve when you know what's really happening for students in assessment conditions. Therefore, you should deliberately plan what you're tracking and monitoring and focusing on.

Geography has specific challenges in this space. We know progress is not linear, and we know that topics often present different 'difficulty' for different students – and exam papers have questions of different types and difficulty. It's also fair to say that many of our skills are synoptic and cumulative in nature: it's very common for students to improve essay writing between Year 10 and Year 11, for example. If we want to plan for 'best bets' or key skills to focus on, or to think about our coverage of skills at a range of stages, a whole curriculum approach allows us to consider how we can use the KS3 curriculum to support.

How do we identify which key issues in geography we want to focus on? There are a number of moments where this process can take place, including:

- Analysis of internal examinations and assessments.

  - Mock exam standardisation. How do we know we've marked the same way? Do we split up marking between the team, or does everyone mark their own classes?
  - How do we plan time to reflect on what we've learned about our students, and get an overview of the cohort and data? Have we all struggled to get positive outcomes on a particular topic, case study, or question type? What does this tell us?
  - What level do you look at as an individual teacher? Do you look at your own class, or across the whole group? Do you debrief as a team? Why? why not?

- External: Once we have real results from GCSEs or A-levels, how do we learn from them?

  - Who does the post-exam analysis? Do you get exam board/ professional feedback, question-level analysis and wider discussions? How is that shared?
  - How do we learn more about how our students did, and what went well? Who is requesting copies of scripts, and how is that formalised and made part of the feedback?
  - How is this information incorporated in to teaching and learning for the next generation of students?

At each stage, it's important to reflect and deliberately ask 'So what?'. What does this help you to change or do differently? How well is it working for your context? How well is it working to improve student outcomes?

It's also vital that we regularly reflect on the cost–benefit of every step. More is not more, and students will benefit from happy and healthy teachers more than a fourth-line analysis of question-level marking and a beautifully formatted spreadsheet!

Teaching is a team sport – and it is also helpful to think about how we share, use and make colleagues, parents and students aware of this wider feedback. Your school context will likely determine the external outputs (e.g., report cycles – written, grades, data drops) or interactions (parent information evenings to support and inform, or parent feedback evenings where analysis and results are shared). There are options for making this as streamlined and efficient as possible, and ensuring that information is contextualised effectively (e.g., Preece, 2019a) but, as with all other feedback, we want to think about how we give people enough information to support the change in outcomes that we're looking for. Student support networks, both inside and outside the school, need to know what is most helpful to make decisions in their context.

> **Critical reflection**
>
> Pragmatically, we should acknowledge the significant burden of multiple exams and demands on student time. Geography is often less likely to be a 'critical problem' from a school, parent or student perspective, and their participation, prioritisation or interventions can often be prioritised accordingly. It can be frustrating to have students tell you that they must go to other revision sessions rather than yours, or that they are going to spend time on their weakest subject rather than pushing themselves to get the best possible geography grade, but this is part of the wider picture of students' performance across the whole curriculum!

How do we do semi-formative assessment in geography?

Research by Roediger & Karpicke (2006) shows that regular testing and quizzing increases the ability of the brain to link information together in a schema, and to recall knowledge. Increased testing under formal conditions, however, can create anxiety and concern in students – together with having high workload implications for teachers.

Low-stakes assessments

The way forward for many has been through the introduction of regular low-stakes quizzing which aims to show links and connections and maximise recall strengthening opportunities. Such quick, often unrecorded, and peer or informally marked quizzes bridge the gap between questioning in your classroom, and summative assessment.

While shared resources can be brilliant, Boxer (2018) has argued that making retrieval practice resources is one of the most powerful tools for developing a teacher's sense of sequencing, critical knowledge, and how to identify learning patterns. There are options which now enable some of this process to be done via an app or website. You can investigate them to establish whether they are right for your context.

Critical reflection

Understanding the infrastructure

When thinking about techniques for any teaching and learning strategy, it's important to acknowledge that every school has a set of factors and infrastructure that can make something work in that specific context. It is tempting to look at someone else's context, and see a superficial feature – for example, the use of app-based low-stakes assessments, or a regular retrieval carousel – and try to use it yourself at that level. Doing so without knowing the infrastructure that sits behind the implementation of that approach, this can be risky. Often, there are a specific set of cultures, factors or developed and reinforced routines that *make it work* for that school – that may be homework policies, tutor or teacher expectations, or a wholescale policy and deliberate investment in a single platform or approach.

As geographers, we should need no invitation to consider the specifics of place more carefully than most, but it's always worth adopting that mindset of professional curiosity above and below the surface when considering things to adapt from other contexts, settings or schools!

Deliberate practice?

Often, to check for geographical understanding, we need a longer answer than a short check of knowledge can give us. A simple recall question can be answered relatively simply and quickly. To check for understanding, we need to understand why and consider options, predictions, and test alternatives.

Sometimes, that means we'll want lots of students giving longer answers – and the most efficient way of doing that, in terms of ratio and time in the classroom, is often to write it down. You might want to assess the answers by walking around doing live marking and making formative comments. Alternatively, you may need to have time to mark and reflect on student understanding at a different stage.

Planning these questions is also important – not just for the impact on lesson time, resources and how you're going to mark and give feedback on them – but also in considering what, and how, you are going to check understanding. It's helpful for you to think about some of the practical considerations for decision-making around these approaches:

- **What are you practising?** Often, there can be a tendency – especially at KS4 and 5 – to default to 'exam questions' – but they only sample a small domain of knowledge and might not really ask the key question for understanding.
- **How do you make it work?** Exam questions written where? On separate paper, in books or mini-whiteboards? Marked how? Marked when, and by whom? How do you remind yourself to ask that question at that moment? This starts to drive your lesson's activities and resources – and should help you to identify what you need to have to deliver the learning outcomes you want.
- **How do you ensure it is an accessible assessment?** Consider how you'll support those who need it: know your students. Be mindful of timings – students need time to think and write, if you are doing written questions – and offering a reasonable amount of silent time is important. Some students will need additional time to process, some will need support with vocabulary, some with writing. Your questions need to be tailored so that you can ensure all of your students have the maximum opportunity to succeed.

Planning your formative assessment and questioning to check for understanding should be part of your lesson preparation and classroom conversation. Doing so helps you understand progress through the lesson, or through key thresholds and sequences of learning in a curriculum.

How do we understand and improve GCSE assessments?

Once we have identified the excellent geography content we want to teach, and planned and sequenced our curriculum for learning, it's essential to have a deliberate strategy for how we will support our students to *apply* that learning under examination conditions.

Understanding the assessment objectives

Although we design a curriculum to be a multi-year journey (three, five or seven, depending on context), we will often teach KS3 classes a 'year at a time' for our KS3. But it's important to think about the whole journey with a Year 10 class. Looking at the whole-course assessment helps you to plan backwards across two (or three) years so you can have high expectations from the first lessons and know where you want to build towards.

Each specification will have its own assessment objectives and approaches to the content. It's worth looking at the details of how the papers are constructed, so that you can get a more granular understanding of what you'll need to teach, and some of the skills you'll want to explore.

- What are the different ways in which knowledge is assessed in the papers? How does that shape the kinds of activities you might want to use in your teaching?
- How do the question papers build towards more complex (or higher tariff) questions? Can you see progression? How might you plan for that in a unit, or in teaching a topic?
- How are the types of assessment and types of question the same across the whole GCSE? Can you see similarities between papers? What might that mean in terms of skills and preparation that you'd need to do? Are there different approaches to different papers that are worth emphasising in teaching, or even in taking a different teaching approach for?
- What range of skills (perhaps even linked to the assessment objectives) do you think are being tested? What kinds of sources, data, images or media are involved? (OS map extracts are common at GCSE, for example!) Are students being asked to simply use and interpret, or to apply knowledge to create them?
- Look at the relationship between the time and the marks available. How many marks per minute? Writing under time pressure, against the clock, is a skill. How might you shape this in your teaching? What might you do to ensure that students are used to working at a similar rate in their written work in lessons, or activities?
- What barriers to learning that aren't anything to do with their geography ability do students face? Think about fluency of reading, writing and literacy limits – and how they might impact students accessing the examination.

- Look at the relationship between the marks available and the space for the answer. What might that tell you about how to frame the length of student responses, or consider the depth of answers?
- What would you expect the grade boundaries to be? What would you want to get for a grade 9? What about a grade 6?
- Are there any components of the specification which are completely untouched in this exam? What does that mean? How do you feel about that?

Having this high-level overview allows you to teach deliberately through the two-year course, with the intent of solving the issues that you have identified for your own context. The balance of curriculum, content and skills and knowledge to be assessed is a vital part of the role of a GCSE teacher, and it's part of how you leverage your geography knowledge and content to get the best outcomes for students.

What kinds of skills and knowledge are assessed at GCSE?

Although each paper and specification will have unique nuances, it's likely that they will assess some common factors:

- Expert subject knowledge of the topics.
- Clear and precise use of geographical terms.
- Confidence with diagrams and representing processes through different forms of explanation.
- Ability to use and interpret source material and data and to re-present data.
- Ability to identify how this could be linked to explorations of fieldwork, or identify the way in which fieldwork can be done to support enquiry approaches.
- Flexible understanding of case studies and spaces which underpins different sections, but most notably in the long-answer questions.

It is common for the papers to be arranged in topics, and for each topic to have an ascending order of complexity. Single tariff specifications usually differentiate by questions through a unit: it is expected that all students will be able to complete the simpler questions at the beginning of the topic, and then, as the questions increase in difficulty, complexity or alternative command words, students will achieve different outcomes based on their work.

To achieve top grades, students will need to be able to score consistently well across multiple topics and papers: to achieve a good overall outcome, they need to be reasonably consistent. Often, the key to success in this area is thoughtful and practised time management.

How do we develop better GCSE outcomes for our students?

Alongside your subject knowledge and confidence with the material, successful GCSE teaching involves a deliberate focus on particular components of skill development, and pedagogical approaches that bring out the best application of geography for our students. There is a subtle difference between teaching really great geography, and teaching in a way that is applicable to exam contexts. Table 16 shows some things you may need to prioritise in your teaching and suggests how you might do so.

▼ Table 16: Skills for students to develop through GCSE

Priority area	Possible actions
Vocabulary and definitions	Make a deliberate effort to teach, model, highlight, review and regularly test vocabulary and definitions. (Ideally, this builds on a solid platform from KS3 – it is a big challenge otherwise!)
	Some teachers like to have 'vocab books' or specific ways of capturing key terminology throughout the whole course – be consistent.
Key diagrams and processes	Know the key diagrams, have excellent models, and ensure students recall and review them regularly.
	Sketch diagrams – particularly on mini-whiteboards – can be an excellent lesson starter recall activity or help to activate learning for a topic.
Factual knowledge of case studies	Promote recall and retrieval of case studies through, for example, deliberate practice at lesson starts, mind maps, or encouraging the development of links between them.
	Consider using a case study multiple times to support building up synoptic understanding and reducing the range of places students are learning about. There are different opinions on this, and you can make up your own mind!

Priority area	Possible actions
Fieldwork skills and confidence	Link to analysis or completion of data or source activities.
	Regularly ask 'How would we investigate that?'
	Remember that fieldwork has its own vocabulary, and incorporate those terms regularly.
Source response	Use different types of information – photographs, maps, diagrams, graphs, charts and statistics – and think about what students are to do with them on a regular basis.
	In England, think about how often OS maps are used to demonstrate location data.
Interpretation or explanation of ideas	Regularly talk and think about different approaches to explanations.
	Students should regularly explain, practise and think about ideas as interpretations and constructions. You may use formal routines (e.g., think–pair–share) or scaffolding to structure this.
	Plan lesson activities that help student become confident in exploring ideas and perspectives – and in drawing on sources, evidence, case studies and facts.
Essay writing	Build up students' confidence in addressing long-answer questions by scaffolding essay planning, paragraph or essay structures and approaches, and then writing against the clock to an appropriate level. This takes time – and is a key part of the two-year journey.

Some of this is 'good geography': it aligns naturally with what we are teaching and how we'd teach it even if it were not assessed. There are other elements of this work that is specific to GCSE-style assessments, and it's helpful to consider that as another strand of teaching. If you are new to a specification, you might want to consider:

- Your personal confidence with the assessment mechanism, knowing how it will appear, or what types of assessment are linked to the content you are teaching.
- Regular exposure to language and decision-making in examinations for your students, so that they know the command words, and know which units will be in what papers.

- Regular timed practice in realistic conditions with the same resources. There is little point practising with lots of notes, or double the time, or a range of scenarios which won't be examined. Students need to get comfortable with being able to work under timed conditions, and get used to reading questions, making plans, and plotting or working with data, as well as writing answers.
- Deliberate planning for assessment and feedback through the curriculum, as a key waypoints on the journey over the two years of study.

Trying to get the best GCSE outcomes might mean very different things for different levels of ability. As you approach the examinations, it's important to focus effort and time where it will do the most good (see Table 17 for some examples) – and to acknowledge that for students, a geography paper is perhaps one out of 30 exams in that season!

▼ Table 17: Approaches to GCSE success

Supporting to achieve Grade 6	Building from Grade 6 to Grade 9
Geography vocabulary: drilling and knowing key terms, and being able to define them.	Fluency of geography knowledge (vocabulary and process) and exam command words.
Exam vocabulary: knowing command words, and what they mean, so they do well in each question they attempt.	Rapid and accurate explanation of core process/diagrams, as a deliberate strategy to build time to write more on essays later!
Focus on low-tariff questions: making sure to get the maximum marks in the first parts of the paper or each question.	Accurate and precise source and response work, so that the medium tariff questions are confidently completed.
Diagrams and 'explain' priorities: being able to do clear and accurate diagrams for the key explanations, and knowing how to annotate them effectively.	Clear explanations and 'pivot' able case studies – so that students are able to develop towards writing fluent essays, and develop 'argument' in their long-answer questions to hit top levels.
Factual / bullet point knowledge of case studies and fieldwork approaches: knowing what case studies apply to which parts of the question, and the key details of each.	Targeted focus on 'weaker' sections, so that students build consistency across all parts of the exam papers.

Supporting to achieve Grade 6	Building from Grade 6 to Grade 9
Scaffolding structures for writing long-answer questions, so that students can apply knowledge effectively. Right decisions on the rubric: knowing what is being assessed, how to make choices, so that students complete the paper, having attempted all questions and not run out of time!	

It's normal to feel like there's a lot of content and information to take in. It takes a while – and sometimes, a philosophical tension or pragmatism – to recognise that being good at teaching 'to the exam' is different from teaching great geography.

How do we understand and improve A-level assessment outcomes?

Most GCSE specifications do not provide opportunities for extended essay writing, so success at this level does not rely on fluency or mastery of essay technique, but rather the consistent delivery of responses to various question types on a diverse range of topics, using different skills against the clock. Assessment objectives shift dramatically at A-level and, to achieve the highest grades, the variety of geographical knowledge is taken for granted.

- A-level objective AO1 combines 'know like a geographer' and 'apply understanding' strands from GCSE into an 'understanding' of concepts, interactions and change.
- Candidates are expected to show mastery of their knowledge, and write for a professional geographer audience, with far more marks available for constructing longer answers.
- Simple structures, like defining terms and key terminology, are far less relevant to the answer. Basic description/narration of the 'geography' of what happens (process, explanation, description of a case study) will probably only get you to the top of Level 2.
- Far more important is the role of 'evaluation' and assessment, and the ability to recognise and construct a viable thesis argument in response to a stimulus (photograph, source, data).

There is – of course – valid reason to practice writing – and getting feedback on – a long-form essay, constructed from paragraphs that flow, particularly against the clock. But, in the early stages of an A-level course, teaching, modelling and practising essay *planning* rather than writing essays, is a quicker and higher-leverage strategy for giving students a sense of what they need to be doing so it has benefits in terms of both time and motivation. Writing solid and detailed essay plans (and building up a bank of them to use as revision) is a far more valuable way to spend time than gradually improving essays.

Why do we teach differently?

To an extent, the foundations of great geography teaching are the same at all levels: expert subject knowledge and clear explanations, grounded in understanding of places and case studies that supports a nuanced interpretation and evaluation of different approaches in different contexts. As a teacher, the first thing you are likely to notice is the deeper subject knowledge required, but the step up from KS4 to KS5 is arguably not as significant a gap as in many other subjects.

The change in assessment is probably what is most important in the A-level teacher's approach – because it drives a different way of thinking, teaching and exploring issues. There is much more appreciation for the richness of complexity, nuance and interpretation at A-level, and successful teachers deliberately plan for that in their approach, rather than trying to add it on afterwards in reflections or essay writing. So, great A-level teaching will:

- Get the foundations right: students need to show mastery of subject knowledge and content. Explanations need to be precise, accurate and fluent, and students need a detailed grasp of processes. Teachers have expert subject knowledge of content and key concepts, and link them together at all stages, combining them with detailed knowledge of case study examples.

- Teaching is deliberately done with complexities and interdependencies in mind. The idea of a 'right answer' or a single interpretation that may have worked at GCSE is limited. Instead, teachers constantly talk about 'factors' or 'priorities' or interpretations. It's common to see debate, discussion and scaffolds to support evaluation of judgements (e.g., diamond nines, washing lines) used frequently as a core part of the teaching.

- Teachers regularly model synoptic thinking – they explicitly make connections to other units and parts of the course, and welcome perspectives from students' lived experiences or other taught courses. What do your A-level economics students have to say about globalisation? What do your A-level historians have to say about causes of conflict, or constructions of global relationships? What do your A-level biologists say about adaptation, or your chemists say about climate change? There is no longer a single narrative, and the connective approach is present in many lessons.

- A common response to student questions is 'it depends'. Teachers and students will regularly discuss what in the space is implicitly comparable, so that they can develop skills to answer the question 'What else could it be?'. As part of that process, students are constantly looking to identify what it could depend on, and how we'd know, or what we could say about it.

In my own A-level teaching career, I developed a number of approaches to deliberately scaffolding this thinking throughout the course. **You can see an example of this in case study 10.1.**

How do we teach evaluation as a skill?

Descriptive or narrative responses will be limited to Level 2 marks, and students need to offer more geographical explanations and evaluation to move towards the higher marks.

But what do we mean by 'evaluation'? Evaluation is a process by which you provide an opinion or judgement about the idea/facts presented, or the question. It will always be a matter of perspective and opinion. This can be frustrating for students, who want 'a right answer', or are more used to structures which allow all essays to be approached in the same way. For many, the development of a responsive approach, where each essay question needs a different structure and response, is the hardest part of the successful transition to A-level.

To do it well, you need to have a clear idea of what you are going to evaluate – and then to provide a clear and logical set of reasons why you've come to that conclusion. One of the approaches that helped in my own A-level teaching was to use core geographical concepts as the framework to explore and experiment with. **In Extras 10.1 you can see how to use geographical concepts to develop good evaluation.**

Building up to this evaluative skill and conceptual confidence takes time and deliberate curriculum thinking. As a teacher, you need to be able to cover the core of subject knowledge content and concepts in detail, with expert explanation of case studies and examples, while also making lesson time available to reflect and develop skills over the course.

The final element of confidence-building in this space is to practice against the clock. Initially, it's once again helpful to teach and model the approach to *essay planning* against the clock – so that students are able to think, evaluate and make a sensible plan under timed conditions. Lots of practice of essay planning – scaffolding at first, then gradually more independent – in 10–15 minute blocks is a much more effective use of lesson time than whole essay creation. **You can see some examples of scaffold development in case study 10.2.**

Once this part has been done well, their essays and writing inevitably flow much better. It's still important to practice the essays themselves – writing for a long period of time requires sustained concentration, and comfort with penmanship! Students rarely write for this amount of time, and it is best to build up to it.

It is also worth reflecting on the 'exam conditions' element of this deliberate practice. Although you will inevitably get a better quality of essay and thoughtful geography if you set an A-level essay as a homework activity, or an untimed exercise, there are limits to what it can tell you about a student's learning. Homework may often include strategies like use of artificial intelligence, sources, reflections, examples and multiple ways of working that simply won't be reflected in assessed conditions. There is value in both, but it's helpful to carefully consider the cost–benefit of each in terms of learning, geography, time and workload for both teacher and student.

Critical reflection

For most students and teachers, geography probably has one of the smoothest transitions between the key stages in terms of learning and content. The cumulative and synoptic nature of our work means that it feels natural for A-level to be more connected and evaluative, and it is probably not as significant or as dissonant a 'step up' between GCSE and A-level as in some other spaces.

> But in this section, it's clear that the change in assessment objectives and style can drive some structural differences in the approach to teaching and learning. You may want to think about how you feel about A-level teaching, and whether you think there is (or should be?) an obvious difference in the way you plan and teach A-level and GCSE lessons. As part of that thought process, it can be helpful to reflect on how you approach the 'culture' for A-level in your context, and what are the potential ways to upskill and develop your A-level teaching if that is important to you.

Whether at GCSE or A-Level, though, it's clear that there's often less separation between geography content and the nature of assessment than we might ideally like. All teachers know about the pragmatic tension between 'great geography' and 'great exam results', and have felt pulled in different directions at stages of their career. It's important that we take a curriculum mindset to this, and develop deliberate and sequenced approaches to building student confidence with examination skills. **You can find some suggestions to develop a curriculum for exam skills in Extras 10.2.**

How do we improve our confidence in our assessment?

The final step of the triangulation needed for the best progress and assessment of exam classes is to build confidence in the reliability of your assessment. This means thinking about how you can standardise and develop your marking – not just in terms of efficiency and feedback, but also in terms of how reliably and consistently you (and your team) are able to interpret and apply assessment mark schemes (see Table 18).

▼ Table 18: Guide to developing exam marking reliability

Before you mark: spend time reflecting on the mark schemes	Pay attention to key differentiators between levels. What must answers include, and what are the key 'hinge' points for answers to move from one level to another?
After you mark: standardise within your department (or trust)	Discussing exam papers and marking gives everyone a better understanding of what other people are thinking, a chance to see a wider range of responses, and ensures all students in your cohort get a consistent experience.

Use examiner reports	If you use a past paper as a mock exam, look at the examiner report. Do your pupils answers show similar patterns to those of the whole cohort who actually sat the paper? You'll be able to spot some areas where you can improve your preparation – and be reassured that your students are like others!
Use exam scripts	Getting papers back, being able to see the marks and provide a WAGOLL (what a good one looks like) example for students in a different cohort is powerful. It's not just about the 'good answers', but sending the message that people in their school – maybe even someone they know – can write like this is inherently building a culture of high expectations!
Professional development courses	Subject associations, exam boards and other organisations offer (paid for) professional development courses that can help you better understand exam requirements.

One route for professional development in this space is to become an examiner yourself. You normally need to be teaching the specification that you're applying to examine for, and you may need to have a certain amount of teaching experience – it depends on the exam board.

Getting good results for our students is a key part of great teaching. It's an important part of professional development to be able to assess effectively, and support students to achieve their potential – even if we might not think of it as the best 'geography' that we can offer. For that, we often want to think about how we take our learning outside of the classroom.

CHAPTER 11
HOW DO WE TAKE GEOGRAPHY OUTSIDE THE CLASSROOM?

Fieldwork is an essential component of geography education, our disciplinary approach and our unique lens on the world. However, it's more than just an academic development. It's about the experience of unfamiliar landscapes, or comparisons with and reflections on your lived experience – helping you move beyond the local environment towards a more global understanding of people and places.

But, as we've seen in recent reports (e.g., Ofsted, 2023; Kitchen, 2025), both the quantity and quality of school fieldwork are under threat. Delivering fieldwork is not easy. In some contexts, we know that students struggle to get outside: there is limited access to school grounds, expensive travel or difficult restrictions in place (beyond Covid pandemic rules). Some locations, contexts and settings are not supportive of a fieldwork experience or programmes of study, and people who do not have the disciplinary context need a justification for the costs. Some teachers are uncertain about how to embed fieldwork into their curriculum and programme of study, while others are less confident in their ability to do all the planning and logistics (Rawlings Smith & Kinder, 2023). Often, teachers and curriculum-makers can find it challenging to describe a progression model for fieldwork and deliberately plan and develop it over time (e.g. Kitchen 2025: figure 13).

Kitchen (2025) shows that fieldwork is more than a simple geographic tool. Figure 1 shows the range of different fieldwork experiences that are often offered and conflated by schools, with a clear differentiation needed in terms of pupil and learning focus. As geographers, we know that fieldwork and outdoor learning often has benefits beyond the specific investigative outcomes (e.g. Kitchen, 2025, figure 2). Our priority should be focused on the geographical experiences of our students, but that does not mean we must only celebrate the distant and novel (Kitchen, 2025: 7). When discussing these issues, it's important to be crystal clear on terminology and expectations, and to understand what we mean when we say 'fieldwork'.

- **Fieldwork** is a core part of the discipline. It's structured, purposeful and involves methodical collection and analysis of data. It's exciting for students to be learning outside of the classroom, but it is just as much part of the curriculum as any other lesson.
- **Field trips** are adventures with geography. You might have an 'awe and wonder' trip to somewhere like Iceland, or a charity project to another country, or even a residential as part of a year-group activity. These are 'nice to haves' – they aren't part of our taught curriculum.

Fieldwork preparation has complex strands that need to be thought about at a curricular level:

- Making the fieldwork purposeful and geographical: planning a sensible enquiry, achieving good results, and learning lots.
- Delivering a safe and well-planned experience: ensuring that the logistics, risk assessments and student wellbeing are all considered effectively.
- Thinking about how you teach in an environment that isn't a classroom.

It's quite common for teachers to focus their time and attention on the second objective. After all, no learning or professional development can take place if the environment isn't safe for the students. But often, the disproportionate administrative burden associated with this work means there's little time left for the others – even though they are vital for the student experience and the teacher's development alike (Kitchen & Maddison, 2021).

How do we make fieldwork inclusive?

Fieldwork is a vital part of doing geography, and we'll talk about planning effective fieldwork from a teaching and learning perspective later. But it's also a big challenge for inclusivity (See Table 19 and Kitchen, 2025: 21–22). Whether it's local fieldwork, awe and wonder trips overseas, or the essential components of NEA and required experiences, geography can sometimes seem like it's full of obstacles for students (Chiarella & Vurro, 2020; Lang, 2022; Maddison & Thurston, 2022).

▼ Table 19: Barriers to inclusive fieldwork

Cost	How expensive is the trip? How does it compare to the students' regular experience, and how are you ensuring all can access it? Are contributions essential or voluntary? Do you have ways of subsidising the cost, or making it as cheap as possible?
Equipment	What assumptions have you made about equipment for participation? Will everyone have appropriate outdoor clothing? Will they have access to waterproof shoes, or good quality outdoor shoes? How will they carry their materials – are they likely to have rucksacks beyond their school kit?
Toilet stops and menstruation	If you organise trips where students won't have easy access to toilet facilities, what are the implications? Are the issues explicitly discussed, or will it provide a barrier to some students in terms of their ability to enjoy and stay hydrated during the day? What about students who may be having their period during a trip? How can you support their experience, and ensure they can participate without barriers?
Unsafe spaces	How do we understand what spaces might be unsafe for our students' experience? This is more likely with residential and overseas trips (though sadly, not exclusively so) where discrimination based on race, religion, gender, or sexuality might be part of local cultures. There are a number of popular fieldwork destinations which have customs based on gender (e.g., women covering heads and shoulders when visiting religious holy sites) or homophobia and the legality of certain behaviours.

How do we overcome the key barriers to fieldwork?

The reasons that actual fieldwork is difficult can sometimes seem obvious, but there's usually a complex interaction of reasons, including:

- Fieldwork places high demands on your curriculum time and skill development.

- Fieldwork is logistically challenging. It's hard to fit into a typical class timetable.
- We live in the UK. The weather is unpredictable at best.
- We don't all live in the same place, with the same access to physical locations. We don't all study the same topics or have the same demands of physical locations in which we need to do fieldwork.
- It costs money.
- Many teachers have only limited experience doing fieldwork themselves.
- Fieldwork poses safety and behaviour concerns different from those in the classroom.
- Teaching in the field employs a different set of skills than teaching in the classroom.
- Many of these are highly specific to different places and cultural and school contexts. Some senior leaders love geography and are fully behind fieldwork being completed, while others need to be persuaded that it's worth the time. Some schools find it very difficult to access the curriculum time, or the transport costs – others find it hard to pick a place!

Ofsted (2023) outlined a disappointing picture for fieldwork:

> Fieldwork was underdeveloped in almost all schools, as the curriculum did not consider how students would make progress in their ability to carry out fieldwork over time. Although COVID-19 had an impact on the number of field trips and visits taking place, fieldwork had rarely been a strong feature of the curriculum before the pandemic. Leaders had not considered how fieldwork should be taught or how students would learn more about how geographers carry out their work.
>
> In some secondary schools, students did not carry out fieldwork in KS3. In primary schools, field trips had often replaced geographical fieldwork. Fieldwork at KS4 and KS5 rarely went beyond the minimum requirements of the exam boards.

This makes no judgement about the range, type or quality of those fieldwork experiences – it simply recognises that there are many schools where fieldwork does not happen and is not an experience available to those students. In the face of these barriers, and this understanding of where many schools find themselves, it's tempting to write fieldwork off as something that can't be done. It's for that reason the Geographical

Association's principles of high-quality fieldwork (Kitchen, 2025: 12) start with the explicit identification of the geographical focus, and integration into the curriculum with clear learning aims. It's important to remember to make use of your support network if you're starting to find challenges: there will often be people out there who have great strategies and tips to help you overcome some of the key problems, in contexts just like yours.

> **Reading recommendation**
>
> Fiona Sheriff's *100 Ideas for secondary teachers: Geography fieldwork* (2024) is an excellent introduction to overcoming several challenges. Packed with simple easy-to-use ideas, and covering a diverse range of topics and approaches, it is an ideal starter to explore ways you can get more fieldwork into your curriculum.

The importance of local fieldwork

One of the greatest fieldwork assets – from a practical, logistical and curriculum experience perspective – is your local area. Fieldwork does not have to be all about exotic and glamorous destinations: the geographic value is in the enquiry, investigation and learning.

Your local area or your school site can provide lots of really fascinating areas to explore further (Sloggett, 2021). As well as being logistically simpler and cheaper, it often has the real curriculum advantage of building directly on students' lived experience (Peppin, 2020): building on their place-based understanding and connection to the area allows them to offer insights and display contextual knowledge that they would simply be unable to access in a 'destination' trip. Although it doesn't work for every type of topic, there are definitely some local-area investigations that will suit your curriculum and the opportunities you have. For example, you might consider:

- Microclimate investigations around your school site (Knight, 2013). Where is it hottest? Where is it quietest? Where are the wind tunnels? You might link this to a specific enquiry question or hypothesis to test (e.g., Which areas of the school are most at risk of flooding?), or a wider thematic approach about sustainability. You could investigate where you would need air conditioning, or how and where you could site solar panels or a heat pump.

- Environmental quality surveys around your school site or local area. Where is it nicest, and why? What makes it like that? Students can create a simple environmental quality survey template and investigate the school itself – which are the best or worst areas for them? You may venture beyond, in to the school grounds, if you have them. You could do 'out of the window' surveys of the local area – look out from the school site to nearby roads or areas to do traffic counts, and then extend the radius of your investigation further.
- How liveable is an area, and for whom? There are some superb examples of 'liveability' environmental quality surveys, which focus on how different people perceive areas. You can reflect on perceptions of diversity or inclusion: How liveable is this area for people who are partially sighted or blind? How liveable would this area be for people with physical disabilities? You could explore social inclusion: How safe do students feel? How much do they feel that this is an area where they can see themselves represented?
- Local-issue investigations are an excellent source of questions and interesting avenues to explore. If there is a local planning debate, building or infrastructure proposal linked to a topic, why not turn it in to a mini-investigation? You can get students to think and design questionnaires and ask people's opinions on the issue at hand. They don't have to leave the school site – you could ask students in form time, staff around the day, or they could take some home to ask parents, for example.
- Linking to a common KS3 topic, you could ask students to complete comparisons where they live, or on their routes to school for almost all these topics, giving an even wider distribution of answers!

For each of these to be geographically effective, of course, they need the same care and curriculum consideration that you'd use to plan a residential trip to the coast. But there is little to no logistical impact of many of these suggestions. You can do them within a lesson, using homework to complete the contrasting location example. You don't need to spend money, travel, or go through your visits approval process (though it's probably always wise to let your department or line manager know you're doing it).

Branching out just a little further, Alcock (2022: 11) suggests that there are other reasons why departments might want to consider using nearby areas – parks in particular – to carry out their fieldwork. These include:

- the impact of travelling on climate change and air pollution
- the benefits of paying attention to place and 'everyday geographies'
- fairer access to field trips, in terms of cost, time and mobility for students
- the ability to revisit locations at different times of day, days of the week, and in different weather conditions
- a lower risk of students leaving the study area, as parks are usually well bounded.

The potential of secondary data and virtual fieldwork

It's increasingly easy to explore the world without leaving home. The rise of digital mapping, virtual worlds, highly effective public data sets and free-to-use websites means that there's much more data at our fingertips than we've ever had access to before. Many teachers will use these tools to 'teach from the front', or illustrate a point or case study example, as we've already seen. But even within the confines of a lesson (Wood & Walker, 2017), you can turn taught content in to an enquiry and investigation on a regular basis. If you treat it in the same way from a curriculum perspective, the use of secondary data to drive investigative and fieldwork skills is an excellent supplemental way to keep skills and thinking current for your students.

For example, you could:

- Use GIS to measure and describe the downstream changes in a river from source to mouth, and explore the cross sections of the valleys and wider drainage basin characteristics (Fryer, 2022). You could do the same with coastal measurements, or glacial surveys, or even dune mapping in the Sahara.
- Use virtual mapping or Street View to conduct environmental quality survey transects in any part of the world. You could compare Rio to Rhyl, or Catford to Casablanca. You can annotate maps with building height and use or density, take transects and samples to compare cities against land-use models, or against different directions from the same centre.
- The same framework could be used to compare areas in terms of urban quality, or start to explore the liveability of areas in the same way as described for the local area, above.

- You could broaden the horizon of 'local-area' investigation to consider national issues like London's Heathrow Airport expansion, or controversial issues in national parks or tourist honeypot sites.
- In the UK context, the publication of the census data allows you to create quite detailed analyses of different areas. You can investigate all dimensions of the data and questions asked – focusing on any number of areas to give real insight into a significant range of human topics.

In many cases, the secondary data experience here would significantly surpass most of the data collection elements possible through a primary fieldwork experience. The reduction of travel, and the huge variety of data, quality and range of questions, and broader spatial options available mean that you could generate meaningful geographical enquiry questions in topics that would not be feasible to plan a visit to.

For greatest leverage, you could potentially combine these two strands to produce exceptional geographical thinking without leaving the school site – comparing your site/local area with another using virtual or secondary data sets. With the right curriculum thinking, there is a rich source of geographical investigations that can be linked to most topics, delivered in most contexts, and provide opportunities to do really stimulating enquiries on a regular basis.

Of course, as geographically sound as these opportunities are, they cannot replace the social, emotional and cultural experiences of getting out of your known and lived experience, and investigating a place beyond the local. But for that, we need to plan and consider trips in a different way.

How do we plan great geography fieldwork?

To deliver great fieldwork – whether virtual, local or more distant – you need to explore the same considerations. This section will focus on the steps we might want to take to think about fieldwork in three stages. The stages have been deliberately arranged in this order: we want to *start* with the geography aims and objectives and then work out how to deliver that safely and in the right environment.

Planning purposeful and geographical fieldwork

As geographers, we know that fieldwork connects learning in the classroom with the complexity of the real world. It is formal education outside of the classroom that involves making hypotheses, testing through observation, collecting and analysing data, and describing findings. The work that we do to explain, explore and justify what we've found is vitally important in making place-based meaning, and in showing students about the way the world works compared to our theories.

Clearly, then, the first part of deciding what to do as 'fieldwork' is whether your curriculum has topics that can be investigated (realistically) in this way, and what places and locations might be suitable and accessible. A UK school can't easily do fieldwork on some topics (e.g., the savanna biome). Other topics (e.g., the changes to an urban area) might be suitable. You might also want to think about when it fits within the school year, to fit best with topics, wider contexts like exams, or the most suitable weather.

These kinds of conversations are ideally had as you are designing and thinking about your curriculum for the year ahead. They need strategic decision-making about the timing of fieldwork relative to other experiences and the demands of the school year, together with consideration of how to embed the learning effectively into a curriculum, scheme of work, or wider journey.

> **Reading recommendation**
>
> Independent fieldwork consultant to the GA, and experienced leader, Chloe Searl has written three separate guides to fieldwork: *Methods of collecting fieldwork data; Methods of presenting fieldwork data, and Methods of analysing fieldwork data* (Searl 2021a; 2021b; 2021c). These offer in-depth thinking and reflections for leaders of fieldwork at all stages. In particular, if you are involved in planning the curriculum, or want to develop your own skills in different areas, these books are an essential read without being unfriendly to the user! Chloe's website (*The Island Geographer*: https://www.theislandgeographer.co.uk/) also contains a vast range of available resources to be used and shared, which can be a huge support for newer fieldwork leaders!

How do you embed fieldwork into your curriculum?

To get the most out of the experience, it is important to teach the procedural knowledge that students need in order to complete fieldwork with rigour. It is also important to teach about the limitations of the methods in geography (something less explicit in many school science investigations) and empower your students to feel ownership of how they are going to investigate the question. None of this happens on a short-term basis – it needs structural and thoughtful design of all three phases shown in Table 20.

▼ Table 20: Planning for three phases of fieldwork

Pre-fieldwork knowledge	Establish the core concepts and knowledge that help put the fieldwork into context. You could set up a 'need to know' through an enquiry approach to a topic, or teach some concepts and ideas and then explore how to investigate them. You could start focusing on the location (or 'case study') that you're going to use, so students start to think about the area, or build some place-based knowledge that helps them connect wider spatial thinking to the specific aspects they are going to investigate.
Skills students need to do fieldwork	You need to think about what you need your students to be able to do, so that they can collect and interpret their fieldwork meaningfully at an appropriate level. What techniques do you need to teach? How do you get them to practice? If the methods and techniques are new to them, how do you rehearse the skills, or develop coherence and standardisation? This reduces the challenges of the 'learning outside of the classroom' experience for you as a teacher too. For example, in developing an enquiry focused on environmental quality surveys, you might want to do some standardisations near the school site, so that all of your class are scoring in approximately the same way, or are familiar with some of the questions. If you're taking students to the coast to do long profiles, then why not take them out to the playground or school site, so they can practice and get confident with a clinometer and break of slope techniques? What numerical, graphical or scientific methods can you link with, so they can make sense of what they have found out?
Follow-up	Once you've got some results, it's important that the students feel like there was a purpose. You might want to make an assessment point; so, they 'write up' their fieldwork and make a project. You might want to turn the results into a classroom display, or a big poster, so that they can see the benefits and outcomes of their work regularly.

Preparation and thinking about the content and topic needs careful sequencing, and the pre-fieldwork methods lessons could easily be two or three separate experiences, too. Generally, the more sequenced the learning, the more deeply rooted the fieldwork process and learning becomes. It can also be a massively important confidence builder for teachers and students who are unfamiliar with fieldwork – which is a huge part of making people feel included – and ensures that there will be few surprises on the day. And, as a final benefit, it changes the dynamic of the fieldwork experience. Rather than having it all to do on the day, you are working with some knowledge and reminding the students of the plan when they step off the coach.

Planning safe and effective fieldwork

Planning and delivering safe and effective fieldwork needs careful consideration of risks. It's probably the area of fieldwork that takes the most time and is of greatest concern to teachers. But 'risk assessment' is a dynamic decision-making process that you are involved in all the time. You judge whether something is dangerous, you assess how you can take steps to reduce the risk – and then either do it, or don't do it.

It's the same for learning outside the classroom. You need to take time to think about what make it difficult for all your students to have a good time, collect great data and stay safe, and then work out if you can take steps to mitigate it. If you are new to leading trips, it's worth talking through your risk assessments and trip plans with a senior colleague who knows the students, or who knows the places. Their support will be invaluable in thinking about how you plan.

Before making any kind of risk assessment, where possible, visit the location in advance (ideally with an experienced colleague): walking the route, viewing the facilities and getting a clear sense of potential dangers is essential for compiling an effective risk assessment. If you cannot visit the location, discuss this with your relevant leadership team. You may still want to go ahead, particularly if you've got experienced colleagues, but it's something to consider.

Once you've had these strategic discussions, you can start to consider some of the smaller-scale risks and approaches that you want to take to them. For a fieldwork risk assessment you should include:

- your students
- individual student needs

- staff support and experience
- emergency actions
- environmental risks
- documenting the risks and keeping the paperwork safe

Extras 11.1 gives more detail about things to consider under each of these headings.

Every school or organisation is likely to have supportive people, advice and guidance about exactly what is required to comply with their own policy. This is the process you need to follow. You will probably have a member of senior leadership or staff who acts as the education visits co-ordinator, and they will sign off and check your risk assessment processes to ensure they comply with your school's requirements. Everyone has their own timescale for this, so do think ahead to ensure you can meet the relevant deadlines.

Dynamic risk assessment

As considered and thoughtful as all of this preparation is, it cannot cover all eventualities. Your plans for the activities, and your prior risk assessments, are entirely theoretical. It is what you do on the day, and how you make those decisions, that matters most. Sticking rigidly to the plan, ignoring changes in conditions that would alter the risks, is just as dangerous as going without any risk assessment at all – and, in most cases, would provide you with as little cover or protection if something went wrong.

It is your responsibility to make decisions in the best interests of the safety of the students and the teachers on the trip – and if that means cancelling activities, significantly changing the day, or coming back with gaps in the data, then so be it.

This is hard. It feels like a big responsibility, and it's probably the bit that is most uncertain and worrying for teachers, particularly if you are less experienced in fieldwork leadership. It's okay to feel that way: every trip I have ever taken has been a privilege, but it's always a responsibility and – for me, at least – that never really changed over time. If you ever get to the point where you are so casual about trip management that you feel like some of the risk assessments, or thinking and planning aren't necessary, then this needs some attention!

Planning for teaching outside the classroom

One of the great joys of fieldwork is that the environment is different to a classroom. You might have a beautiful backdrop to your lesson; you might have new and exciting sounds or things to catch the eye. You may also have more challenging conditions. It might be cold, or raining. You might have some grumpy students who've done more walking than they anticipated, or who didn't bring the right equipment, and now they're a bit sore.

So why do we assume that our regular classroom teaching techniques and methods are going to translate to this new space? Often, we don't really think about how we're planning to talk, teach and manage student activity until we turn up, until we're faced with the immediate decision-making of 'Where do I stand? Where do I put them?'. That's challenging and stressful – ideally, you can plan and prepare some of this in advance. Table 21 shows some things to think about.

▼ Table 21: Planning to teach outside the classroom

Using your voice	It sounds really obvious, but outside is not the same as being in a classroom. It's noisier, windier, and sound will just fade away.
	Think carefully about positioning students so they can hear you.
Positioning and grouping students	As well as thinking about how well students can hear you, think about what they're looking at. Facing a view, or the landscape and space you're describing, is positive but can be distracting.
	Do you get them to grab a seat on the nearest suitable space? How do they do that?
	You may want to have a 'hold point' where you do the initial briefing or teaching (could even be on the coach), so you can then have attention the best way.

Resources and visuals	If you've got something critical to show, or something like a field sketch to do, then it's unlikely that anyone can see the A4 version you've got. So, I'd strongly encourage you to generate a fieldwork booklet that contains any key resources, and spaces for questions, notes, work and development. If you have non-specialist staff joining the trip to help out, a booklet can be really powerful to help them connect with the activities, learning and key outcomes they're looking to support. It's a great framework for the staff briefing, too.
How far is too far for 'classroom circulation'?	In an ordinary lesson, you'd set students off on a task, and then walk around to see how they were doing. In a fieldwork setting, they might be significantly more dispersed. Think about how you might plan to use your wider staff team here. Do you have one per group, for example? What are they looking for and supporting with? Geographers may know, but your non-specialist staff often might not.
Communicating time and activity changes	How do you plan to let groups know how long they've got, and when to come back? This is either something that's a vital part of the pre-briefing before they start an activity, or something that you need to think about managing during the activity.
Contingency planning	If you turn up at the location and it's hammering down with rain, you might shift the activities around. You might move the 'classroom instruction' bit indoors, or into a space where you can find some shelter first. It's important to factor the 'quality of learning and teaching' in to the 'risk assessment' bits – you have to balance the need for learning and outcomes in to your thinking.

As well as these practical and pedagogical thoughts, it's worth considering the human and performance factors, too. Over the course of a day, you must teach and lead for a long time. You need to think about hydration, energy and nutrition. Know what works for you, and what signs and symptoms indicate you are flagging or feeling a bit tired. Pack some sweets or treats. Get your colleagues to remind you about drinking, and remind them. If you can, figure out the 'downtimes' where you can rotate a quieter section of work through the team, or spaces where you know you can grab a little time for a drink and a mental breather.

You can see a common theme emerging through all of these threads. Fieldwork is so precious that we need to get it right – and have it thoughtfully and carefully embedded in our curriculum work. If we can do that, then a series of the geographical questions can be considered at the planning stage – but so too can some of the practical steps to develop great skills and practical experience, design good resources and frameworks to carry out the fieldwork, and bring great data back with us.

Fieldwork is iterative for us as teachers – we learn from it each time, get better at the teaching outside the classroom, and develop our skills in planning and leading great geographical experiences. For our students, it's less likely to be iterative. They might have amazing geographical, or socially and culturally transformative experiences (e.g., Cook, 2010), and we want to make sure that impact is as powerful as it can be. For some of our students, it might be the moment they realise the amazing nature of geography and decide to study it further! For some of our students, particularly at A-level, it may also be a significant component of their assessment and coursework demands, and they have to make the most of that.

Assessing fieldwork: the NEA requirements

In previous iterations of the curriculum (Gardner, 2022), student-led fieldwork investigations formed parts of the examined experience at both KS4 and KS5. Controlled assessment was removed from GCSE geography in the 2018 specification reform, and a modified version put into the A-level specification as the NEA (Kitchen 2025: 19).

The student-led nature of the NEA reduces, in principle, a number of the practical and logistical issues of delivering fieldwork for the school and teacher. The onus is on the student to conduct the investigation independently – though many schools still provide some supportive frameworks, or locational support to do investigations.

What has become more critical for schools is the need to have a curriculum mindset and progression framework for fieldwork over time. There is rarely time to develop all of the skills from scratch in Year 12, and it is important that much of the curriculum and disciplinary principles of enquiry and fieldwork have been embedded well before that. Even if you rely on experts to support and deliver the fieldwork data collection experience, the wider thinking by students is a vital part of their success.

In **case study 11.1, independent field studies tutor Chloe Searl** reiterates the importance of the curriculum mindset for fieldwork, and the need to thread skill and enquiry development through the geography experience at every key stage. It should be clear that this is not just 'nice to have' – a thoughtful and progression-focused approach to fieldwork is directly correlated to student success and outcomes.

It's worth thinking about how you 'assess fieldwork' further down the school, and the extent to which you make this an explicit part of your curriculum planning and progression model (e.g. Kitchen, 2025: 20 shows embedded methods and retrieval practice using fieldwork multiple-choice questions). Would you ask students to present their findings in a particular way? To justify their outcomes, or evaluate their methods and data? Why not integrate some of these thoughts and strands in to fieldwork at all levels, and encourage students to reflect on the richness of participation and evaluation, rather than simply analysing the data? Like geographical enquiry, it's important to show students that we can close the loop and answer questions completely and fully.

The aspiration for the NEA to be the peak of a students' geographical experience is a positive idea. The practicalities of delivery – and the time taken for assessment, moderation and marking to be concluded – have probably left most teachers less enamoured of it than their students. As with every assessment, the balance of practical, equitable and disciplinary fidelity is a constant judgement call that every school and teacher will find a different answer for.

While there have been significant developments for geography's curriculum content and representation in recent years, fieldwork remains one of the bigger challenges for schools to solve. Ofsted's report (2023) shows that too many students are not getting opportunities to participate in fieldwork, and making it high quality, progressive and thoroughly embedded in our curriculum will take significant national and collective effort to solve. The wider landscape – including the challenging educational picture, and the cost-of-living crisis – means that delivery of high-quality fieldwork experiences is variable at best. If we want to continue to attract students to study geography, and to do it well, then we must make substantial steps forward in this area soon.

How do we plan for great field trips?

Where possible, it's the adventures that geography can take you on that inspire the students well beyond the curriculum. The benefits can go well beyond the connection to the subject – field trips can be personal, emotional and culturally enriching journeys that remind us why we teach young people. In **case study 11.2, Karen Corfield from Discover the World Education** shares why they are so important to aim for us as geographers and teachers.

These adventures can often be what leaders or parents imagine when they hear 'fieldwork', but having a clear understanding of the purpose of such trips is vital if you want to offer them (Kitchen, 2025: 7). They should never be compulsory, nor should they be part of the marketing of geography as an academic options choice. Having separation between the fieldwork we need, and the 'holidays with geographers' that we want, helps us to make the case for each of these things separately.

Whether they are 'awe and wonder' day trips or residential trips, these are often significantly more expensive and more complex to plan and deliver so they are a substantial undertaking for the trip leader. Often, that is partly alleviated by the use of expert external providers – who take on the logistics of accommodation, flights, passports, or international travel options in-country – but these inevitably add significant costs for participants.

With our inclusion and equitable perspective on geography, these can often be divisive. It is important, too, to acknowledge the carbon footprint and impacts of international travel, and to make a personal judgement about the benefits and costs of trips in this way.

But what a case to be made! For the lucky few, their impact can be truly transformative. Delivering an awe and wonder trip – even if it's only UK based – is a significant ask. Much of the thinking that has gone in to developing fieldwork planning skills is relevant here, but there are some other things it may be useful to think about:

- Don't underestimate the administrative burden involved.
- Timing is essential. Because of the scale of the trip, and often the associated costs, trips and adventures are often planned and set up multiple academic years in advance.
- Do lots of research, and think carefully about providers.

- You need to think about how people will pay. Unlike most day trips, it's likely that you'll need to offer instalments as an option for parents.
- Choosing the right staff team for the trip – leadership experience, qualifications, and shared understanding – is vital for success.
- Briefing and explanations are more critical for big trips and big costs than day trips.

Further considerations are explored in Extras 11.2.

Done well, these awe and wonder experiences can genuinely be life-changing moments that students and staff will always remember. There is a huge burden to delivering them well, and a lot to consider, but they can be amazing for your professional and personal experience (Snelling, 2015).

When I started my teaching career, I was hugely fortunate to work in a school where the head of department had built a culture of fieldwork and field trips. **John Snelling describes his philosophy in case study 11.3**, but how did it work in practice? With a curriculum of academic progression and development, the enquiry and skills components were thoughtfully developed at each stage. Through every year of the school, the fieldwork and field trip offering was not just a geographical learning experience, it was life experience. The curriculum mindset deliberately cultivated not just the academic development of the students, but their confidence as citizens, people and travellers. From humble beginnings in local-area exploration of London, there was a mindset of building confidence to take public transport, talk to locals, learn a little language and try a little local culture. By Year 13, they could even plan independent work in a different city, and we could treat them with the adult respect they had earned.

Not all schools design a curriculum which embeds a vision for fieldwork in the same way, or with the same levels of expertise and ambition. But it's important that we think about what fieldwork and field trips can mean for us, and for our students, beyond the specification and the subject. They offer genuine life-changing moments, if we can make them.

CHAPTER 12
HOW DO WE TAKE GEOGRAPHY BEYOND THE CURRICULUM?

The best 'beyond the classroom' experiences are often driven by a mixture of external expectations and internal interests and passions. You might have a keen interest in something and offer it – or students might approach you to lead a club on the thing they care about. These experiences and relationships can be a huge source of professional joy and pride: often, teachers enjoy these clubs because it reminds them of the reasons they love their subject or their school community.

Sometimes, extracurricular activities are 'associated' with a subject, rather than because of an emerging demand. For example, because we know our way around fieldwork and maps, it's often assumed that we'll want to lead Duke of Edinburgh's award (D of E) or adventurous activities. Or, because we teach about climate change, it's presumed that the geography department will lead on the school's sustainability plans or activities. These come with judgements about what geography – department, teacher and subject – means. If you agree with them, and are happy with them, then it's a good fit. If you don't, then it's important to explore that before taking it further! It can be helpful to frame such decision-making in some terms that are common to us as geography teachers.

Your sustainability is vital. How do you manage your workload and wellbeing? For some, extracurricular activities – time consuming as they are – are the things that bring them the most joy in a working week. For others, the burden of planning, admin and responsibilities might make it far less worthwhile. Running a lunchtime society where students do lots of the work is clearly a different ask to overseeing the D of E, for example. Know what works for you, and how you judge extracurricular participation as part of that.

This means – as with our case studies – a careful cost–benefit analysis. You might get paid to lead a more complex activity, and that might be worth it for you at this moment in time. You might be taking the lead on a whole-school initiative that you think will be great for your career progression. You might be running something that brings you great personal satisfaction or joy.

It's important that, when you make your decision, it fits with your values and your needs. Consider:

- What brings you joy, and what aligns with your own values? If it's good for you, and you enjoy it, then the sustainability benefits are higher!
- How much time and commitment is really involved? Like teaching, we know that it's not just about the time 'in the activity' – does it requires significant planning, preparation, admin or substantial weekend and holiday commitments?
- How do you get proper support for the activity? Will it be resourced, have timetable time allocated and be funded? Will it fit with what your school wants to offer, or align with other people's values and priorities?
- How do you make it live beyond you? Creating a sustainable activity means thinking about succession plans and distributed leadership. No matter how much you care about the theme, or believe in the values, you must figure out a way to bring student leadership (and more staff) on board so that it becomes something that is part of the culture of the school.

As ever, your context and conversations in your place and with your communities are vital. When considering options and activities that could be offered, it's worth reflecting on how some key questions relate to your context. For example:

- What is the societal/wider perspective of 'geography' and what it connects to? What expectations do people have for the role of geography in society? How are these factors experienced in your school or context?
- What expectations do students have for careers or pathways in geography?
- What expectations do parents have for the activities and provision of geography outside of the curriculum? This is normally linked to field trips rather than clubs and societies within a school day, but it's worth being aware of how parents see your subject!
- Which areas are most naturally associated with geography in terms of overlap for extracurricular activities?

Creating a culture of geographical scholarship

To really bring geography alive in our classrooms, we must create a culture of scholarship around the discipline. From a practical perspective, scholarship means:

- Respecting and embracing the discipline as a way of seeing the world and exploring the big issues that we face.
- Understanding that geography is a massive and diverse subject, and that it's okay to have interests and things you really like within it. You don't have to be an expert in every part of it.
- Acknowledging that we are all still learning, and that there is constant change and renewal in theory and practice.
- Appreciating the cultural importance, and academic value, of lived experience and contributions from all.
- Actively modelling good questioning, academic curiosity and learning as part of our regular engagement and conversations with students and each other.
- Celebrating and sharing these conversations and experiences, so that they become normalised and part of the 'diet' of our students' learning.

The biggest asset that any department has are the teachers. Having enthusiasm, sharing the knowledge and excitement about the world and the content we're teaching, is what makes geography come alive.

Some schools will have structures they use to model this (for example: 'I'm currently reading' on classroom displays, or on email signatures), but you can consider and take your own approaches to this. In terms of teaching and learning experiences, it's important to consider:

- **Reading and awareness of scholarship and debates.** How does your curriculum explore or encounter debates in geography, and how do you shape those with your students when they come across them?
- **Critical perspective on 'right' answers or complexity.** The older your students get, the more the 'right answer' should be 'it depends'. It needs to be embedded in your daily teaching and learning habits to be truly effective: it never quite works when you try and rush it all at the end as some kind of synoptic conclusion.
- **Access to the highest-quality debates, discussions and speakers and thinkers.** Ours is a diverse discipline with many experts. Building a

culture of scholarship means hearing from more than just the teachers in the team. Seeing teachers sit in the audience as a learner is a powerful modelling experience. You may have parents or contacts who can come and speak at your school. You may be able to work with local schools, hubs, trusts or nearby universities or agencies to get some kind of partnership and experience in a related field – perhaps the Environment Agency, or a nearby green employer? Several universities have 'subject knowledge updates' for teachers, where academics deliver online lessons and resources that support a particular theme. You might be able to spend money on RGS schools membership and share the Monday-night lectures with your students.

- **Access to the highest-quality resources you can get.** Showing that the discipline is constantly changing, and there's lots explore, means having insight into what students could read, watch or think about. For example, at the end of each budget year, if there was any money left over, I'd buy some books: from the *Very short introductions* series (excellent for academic grounding and consideration of key issues) or 'popular geography' books, or texts from first-year undergraduate reading lists (these offer a deeper understanding than our A-level syllabus), or something to give an enthusiastic student a chance to delve further in to something that had grabbed them. Over time, we had built up quite a library – perfect for saying 'Oh, you are interested in X: have you thought about reading Y?' at the end of a lesson, or (more pragmatically) when the students came to talk about how to develop their UCAS statements. In recent years, with virtual learning environments, we also compiled lists of good videos, TED talks, explainers, debates and podcasts. If you can, you might want to offer students the chance to subscribe to some of the excellent publications available, such as *Wideworld* (https://www.hachettelearning.com/geography/wideworld-magazine).

- **Encouraging students to have a voice in geography, and to use it.** This might involve supporting and promoting geography-based EPQs, for example, or considering supporting students with entries to the Young Geographer of the Year or *Financial Times* essay competitions. At the highest level, you may want to encourage students to write articles for *Routes* (https://routesjournal.org/about/about-routes/) and experience the process of academic writing and peer review.

I think things like this are at the heart of a great geography experience for students. It's critical for the wellbeing of a department that the academic energy, enthusiasm and joy goes well beyond the prescribed curriculum.

Creating, sharing and actively celebrating that culture of scholarship is at the heart of successful geography teams, and makes a huge impact on choices, participation and buy-in from students and parents alike. It may even lead to higher results outcomes – but that's not why we do it.

Extracurricular geography

As a result of the diversity of interests within geography as a subject, as well as the experience and background of our geography teachers, there's often a huge range of activities and extracurricular visits that can be led or run from geography departments. This list gives some examples, but is not exhaustive.

- Many schools have student societies. They might be a space to give talks or discuss key events, perhaps with older students leading or presenting and younger students participating. They might be an activity-led space where you build model volcanoes or do related projects that are just beyond Mode B teaching. Such interest-led societies may require co-ordination or resource provision, but often have only a gentle impact on teacher or department workload (Davies, 2020): the best societies require only minimal supervision because the older students lead the activity and do the work!

- Both Amnesty International and Model United Nations offer a more structured and involved approach, focused on international engagement and active student membership. They may well often overlap with other humanities subjects, including history and politics.

- 'Green Club' or some form of sustainability society may sit with geography or biology or wider science. These are often student-led societies with a focus on responding to climate change in some way – involvement in projects around the school site, or some kind of campaigning and awareness work. The most structured approach is to enrol in an accredited scheme (e.g., Eco-Schools, https://www.eco-schools.org.uk/), which can lead to recognition and quality marks. While this kind of society may well have student leadership or initiatives at the heart, success and impact is often reliant on engagement with the wider school community, in particular those with the ability to make meaningful change. If you can get your leadership and finance teams onside, it will be a powerful experience for the students and the school alike.

- Several schools have gardening, growing or planting societies. I've seen some schools work with the RHS Campaign for School Gardening (https://www.rhs.org.uk/education-learning/school-gardening), which is effective. It needs resources, time and expert leadership so is often staff-led and directed.
- An orienteering club may connect the PE and geography departments, and I've seen this run as a spring/summer activity. It's a non-starter in some places – the lack of courses and extensive support networks makes it difficult to do by yourself.
- As already noted, geographers are often involved in D of E schemes in school. Whether it's supporting with route planning, preparation, training, or supervising and taking part in expeditions, a successful programme tends to only work with a relatively large number of sympathetic staff. The planning elements overlap with the way we do fieldwork, so it's common to see shared skills or resources (e.g., maps, compasses). Running the scheme as an administrative role is a significant ask, and leading expeditions in the field is best done with support and, ideally, some form of professional training or outdoor leadership qualification.
- In some schools, there may also be an adventurous activities programme (climbing, trekking, overseas expeditions). As with D of E, these are amazing opportunities, but they tend to require significant investment of time, personal skill and qualifications, and work best when they are naturally aligned with the hobbies or experience of a leading member of staff.

CHAPTER 13
HOW DO WE SUPPORT STUDENTS TO CHOOSE GEOGRAPHY?

Although we may sometimes wish otherwise, geography is an options subject in most schools in the UK. This means that we need to actively consider how we encourage students to continue with their geography studies at key decision-making points within their journey. How this is done always depends on context: you need to know how choices are made, and the processes and stakeholders that operate, so that you can offer the most effective support for your students.

Understanding the context, process and the key stakeholders

Nationally, geography is on the rise. Uptake at GCSE has increased steadily to nearly 300,000 over the past decade, driven by the EBacc and the hard work of teachers in addressing real-world issues. There has been significant growth in students of minority ethnic or economically disadvantaged backgrounds (RGS, 2020), who have not traditionally studied or considered geography as an option.

However, A-level entries are less steady. Nearly 250,000 students who studied at GCSE do not take up A-level. Fewer still are continuing to university: only about 9000 students accepted offers for geography, Earth or environmental science degrees in 2023. At A-level and university level, geography is significantly less economically and ethnically diverse (Dorling, 2019), which is of concern when addressing the issue of whose geography we are representing or teaching. Despite evidence to the contrary, geography at A-level or degree is not perceived as high-earning or high-status (RGS, 2020), and this has significant impact on who chooses it. Dorling (2019) argues that it becomes a luxury subject – studied only by those for whom academic interest is more important than the economic cost or perception of future career outcomes, or by those who see the social and cultural opportunities as a benefit, not a barrier. Inevitably, with a demand for geography-related degrees as a pre-requisite for most teacher training pathways, this has a significant impact on what geography teachers of the future will look like, too.

This may be completely different in your setting. You may have high conversion from GCSE to A-level, or send a significant number of students to university each year to study related degrees.

Whatever the case, it's important to consider who has a stake in the decision-making – all those shown in Table 22.

▼ Table 22: Stakeholders in decision-making for options

Students	They will have preconceptions and experiences created by your previous curriculum, together with wider influences from other subjects, their peers and family, and wider considerations (especially higher up the school, where careers and university decisions become more research-informed).
You and your department	Are the team all enthusiastic and confident promoters of geography? Do some people always have loads of students signing up, and what can you learn from them?
	Do students and parents have confidence in your department to deliver results? The best departments tend to have stable relationships with students, so that they are known and trusted, and they are confident in the trajectory and outcomes of students in the subject.
	If you have great GCSE results, or lots of students going on to university, how are you promoting, celebrating and making that obvious to the Year 9s sat in your classrooms?
	How are you ensuring parents are confident that you will be able to support their child to whatever level of success they want?

Your school and senior leadership context	When are students making options choices – formally, and informally? When are you able to talk to students about the factors?
	Do you have some kind of options evening to share information with a wider audience?
	Are they choosing between different 'blocks' in a timetable/EBacc setting, or do they have a free choice?
	What tends to happen in your context? Are there successful departments that you need to learn from, or consider how you message your choices discussion against?
Parents and carers (often far more significant than we think!)	When parents think about the geography they learned, they might be less inclined to support or see the relevance – their experience of geography is likely to be substantively different to that of their children.
	How might messaging what is being taught and why, feed into considerations of what is a 'viable option'?
	How do you ensure that there's a genuine understanding of the relevance and subject in your context?
	Understand and acknowledge any vocational pressures grounded in parental and community contexts – expectations to follow a career-focused pathway, to study 'valuable' subjects that lead to a higher-paying job, or to not to study beyond GCSE etc.

It's also important to acknowledge the range of curriculum and wider experiences that contribute options choices (see Figure 7). The timing, process and context for decision-making will be different for every student, even if the whole cohort goes through the same procedure! Some make decisions as early as the end of Year 8, when their assessments give an idea of 'what they're good at', and will disengage all through Year 9, well before options have been formally chosen. Others are narrowing down options all through spring of Year 9, and the type of lessons and content you're doing at that moment might be critical.

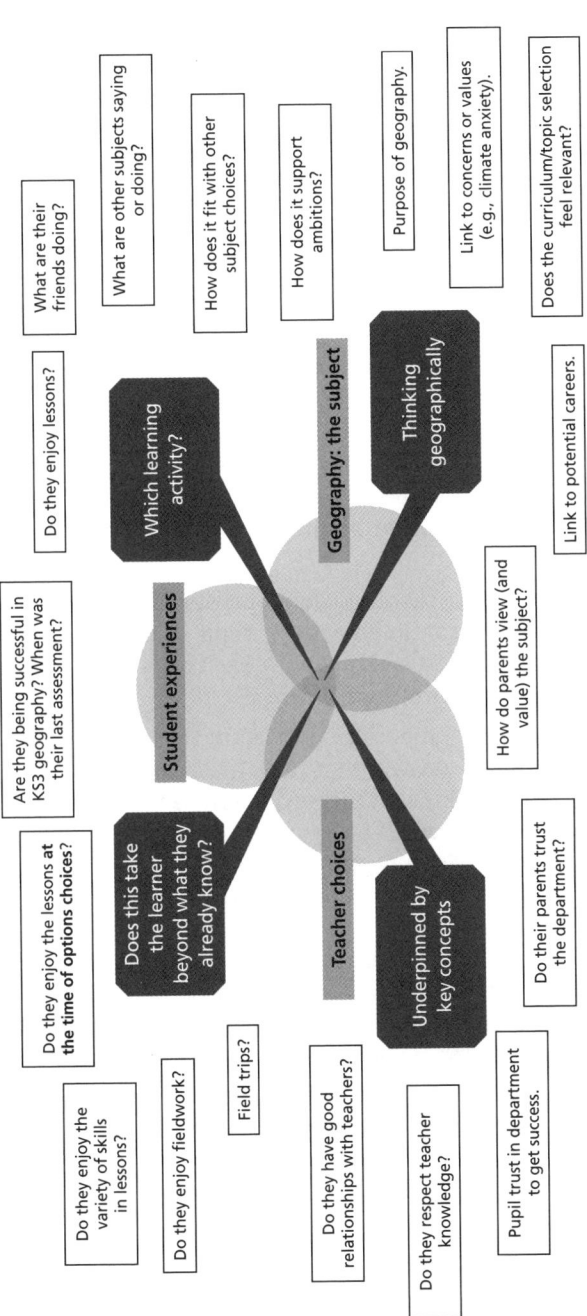

▲ **Figure 7: Some considerations for GCSE options choices**

Figure 7 shows that the layers of the intended curriculum quickly spread through stakeholders to a much wider range of enacted and experienced curriculum outcomes. How well do you know these, and understand what's used as decision-making in your context?

Supporting GCSE options

Once you know your context and understand the conditions in which students are making their options choices, you need to:

- Understand the timing and parameters: know when the options are submitted, when the conversations really start, and how to support and consider the messaging in between. We used to have drop-in conversations in January, ahead of an options evening in February. We'd have an end-of-term assessment in December, and the grades and marking of those were critical – being able to say 'you've done really well in this, and it's a similar standard to GCSE' was key in ensuring high options take up.
- Carefully consider what you're teaching when options time occurs. Is it exciting? Complex? Grown-up and showing insight in to the world? If you're doing a topic that's not crackling with exciting and relevant geography, then consider swapping your timings!
- Show the variety of skill development. It's important to give messages about 'how we do geography' rather than just 'what we study'. The mixture of thinking, analysis, skills, numeracy, graphicacy and writing is a positive thing. Your lessons won't be heavy on essays and reading about lots of different topics. They won't always get the same thing, and the day-to-day of 'life as a GCSE student' in your lessons will be a key attraction. If your KS3 lessons and curriculum are doing their job, they'll know this already. Sometimes, it's worth getting current GCSE/A-level students to come and talk to your Year 9s about what it's 'really like'. This helps support decision-making about the kinds of skills and subjects that work and go together.
- It's helpful to show that there's not a major jump from KS3 to KS4 in difficulty. Know your context well: for some, the repetition of content can put people off, for others, it's really reassuring and supportive.
- Showing value and connections all the way to A-level is important for some – most often the parents. It's less directly linked to university and careers at this stage, but often about 'keeping doors and options open' for A-level choices.

- Increasingly, we are recognising value of being 'green' or 'sustainable', and students desire to be involved in key net-zero careers. If you feel you know little about these, the RGS careers resources (https://www.rgs.org/schools/resources-for-schools/choose-geography-careers-resources) are definitely worth checking out.
- It's important to think about how you are constantly demonstrating your department's knowledge, expertise and successes – particularly to give parents maximum confidence in the journey and support for success. If you have impressive results, where are they displayed and shown? If members of your team are examiners, are involved in subject associations, or have written textbooks, how are you ensuring that this expertise and experience is shared with students and parents?

There's a temptation to see this as a zero-sum game and, at times, it's likely to feel like that. But we all genuinely want to get the best outcomes for our students and sometimes that will mean advising them to choose something else, or accepting that a potentially brilliant geography student will choose another option. Try and be honest about values and fit: you want great students who want to be there, and care about what you offer. There are always trade-offs between the number of students, the enjoyment of classes, and the final outcomes and results. You must balance these carefully in your context.

Supporting A-level options

As students approach A-level options, the landscape shifts a bit more. Personal conversations about values, careers, ambitions and subject combinations are more critical. While some students may take on an EPQ alongside the typical three A-levels, this transition marks a considerable reduction of the breadth of a students' study focus! Choices are a much more deliberate action: they are less likely to be boxed in by EBacc or timetable constraints. It's likely that you'll have a longer deliberation window – although, often, at the same time as students are feeling pressure to learn and perform in their GCSE exams, in a way that they did not at KS3. This is worth balancing and considering – how do you make it as easy as possible for them to be confident and feel supported in the options process?

- The narrowing of the A-level pathway often focuses attention on Stem or the perception of choices which lead to a high-value career (medicine, law etc.). This may well come from the students, or the wider community and parental context. Challenging this narrative is difficult, and often it is more helpful to focus on the ways that geography can facilitate other choices and offer a complementary set of skills to most pathways. You need to be clear about your course, and exactly what it offers in terms of skills, development and big ideas, not just list the units of the specification!

- It's likely that A-level choices have a sharper focus on success. Students don't just want to know what they can study, they want to know how likely it is that they will do well. Confidence in department knowledge, subject expertise and success is vital to build here – how do you celebrate, demonstrate and prove (or improve) that track record?

- Increasingly, A-level choices are about the wider context rather than just the curriculum. We know that motivation, wider reading and doing additional work is vital for sixth-form success. How do you build on the themes of scholarship and empowerment in your department, and model student interests and ownership as something to aspire to throughout your A-level experience?

- At GCSE, the focus is often about enjoying the subject as an endpoint. By A-level, some students are starting to think more carefully about where it might go in the future. It's helpful to have a sense of careers connections, and work with your knowledge of careers and university pathways. Students appreciate support and advice that is grounded in experience and expertise.

You can significantly develop your skill and expertise in supporting students to choose A-level by understanding your context and place well. How do your students and parents feel about some of the bigger issues here? Do they see university as a place for people like them? Do they focus on certain types of career or pathways? Are there nearby industries with significant green or net-zero links where geography can clearly be signposted?

The RGS *Choose Geography* resources (https://www.rgs.org/choose-geography) offer great insight and support. They are free to download and explore, and there are often events, workshops and webinars about choices, careers and pathway options.

Supporting geography at university

One of the great privileges of teaching in an 11–18 context is the ability to hand the baton on to our higher education colleagues, and support young people in becoming geography students at university. But, in my opinion, university and UCAS advice is also one of the most common 'tacit knowledge' areas for teachers. Rarely do you get professional development, support or training on the process to help you understand how it fits together, and the part you play in each of the different steps. It's important for you to keep asking questions and developing your knowledge of the process as well as the individual areas of subject and how it works at university level.

Teaching is a team sport: and especially so when it comes to careers advice at this stage. You need to work closely with sixth-form tutors and your leadership team, and stay connected to the processes, systems and timelines of your setting. Everyone does it a little differently, and you've got to balance subject considerations with wider responsibilities to your students. So, as a geographer, what do you need to think about?

- Recognise that 'geography' is very different at university. Degree options are much wider than the 'human, physical, fieldwork' division at GCSE and A-level suggests. There are a range of courses (human or physical focused) and related subjects (Earth science, environmental science, geology, development studies, international relations) which can be hugely appealing and empowering for students who have developed interests in certain themes. It can sometimes be a little overwhelming, too, so support and guide them by asking research-informed questions.

- When choosing a university geography course, students need to research to understand the nature of the course, what it offers, and the way it works. Some have fieldwork and exotic trips. Some offer dissertations. Some offer assessment through all three years, others offer coursework, or final exams. Students must get into the detail to find what is right for them.

- You may get asked to provide practical and coaching support as a student prepares their personal statement. That might be reading and commenting on drafts, or supporting and coaching the reading and development of scholarship that will be fed into it.

- Many of these support and guidance processes are magnified if a student is considering an application to a high-tariff university (e.g., Oxford, Cambridge, Durham, LSE). It's important to acknowledge and understand the additional processes and pressures on the student and the supporting staff (Preece, 2022). Make use of the wider team in your context to find out more and get support or help with practice interviews and technique.

This list demonstrates just how important it is to recognise sixth-form advice as a specialised area. As well as knowing your students, your context and your communities, great champions in of university geography need to develop their understanding of the complexity and diversity of the subject offering. It's not enough to have done a geography degree some (many) years ago –we need to recognise that our experience is time- and place-limited, and that we need to stay current and reflective if we are coach students.

In **case studies 13.1, 13.2 and 13.3, Sadie Pither, George Zarkos and Sinem Ishlek** give their perspective and advice to teachers, after studying A Level Geography at school. They've all taken very different pathways in geography and later careers and have a range of interesting points to make! However, the importance of conversations and discussions is a common thread. They are particularly vital for the young adults who are exploring all kinds of decisions, at a pressured and difficult time of personal and academic transition. The earlier, more regular and more coaching-oriented your conversations are, the less stressful and lower-stakes the experience will feel for all.

As much as I'd encourage you to learn more, and become more confident in having the conversations, it is always essential that you step back and listen to the students' ideas. They need to be directed to research and really explore their ideas thoughtfully. You can support and encourage, but the decisions need to be theirs.

Supporting geography careers education

Previously an under-resourced area of the wider pastoral development of students, careers education, information and guidance is now a vital part of ensuring that all pathways are effectively supported, considered and explored. It is likely that specialists will form part of your wider school team, but it's important to understand how and where you can play a role in careers education as a geography teacher.

Dorling (2019) argues that university geography is often the preserve of wealthy middle-class – and predominantly white – students. The 2020 RGS report suggests that lots of students choose their A-levels based on the perception of careers and the salary they think they might be able to earn. This is particularly true of first-generation university students, or students from particular ethnic groups *and their parents* (Brace & Souch, 2020; Hesslewood, 2023). This is why it's so critical that you appreciate and understand the personal context in which your students are making options choices, and are aware of the community and stakeholder contexts that are important to help them constrain or make choices.

The changes to GCSE and A-level options entries for students from disadvantaged, and ethnic minority backgrounds are creating that white middle-class cohort that Dorling (2019) described. We have to recognise that focusing on 'transferable skills' or economic arguments can just reinforce Dorling's pragmatic acceptance that many bright geography graduates end up in a commercial city, law, banking or management consultancy career.

There is a perception problem in terms of what careers geography makes available. While some students find the 'traditional' careers – town planning, mapping or geography teaching – attractive, they don't capture the imagination in the same way as careers in sport, arts or science may do (Hesslewood, 2023). The connection between geography and university disciplines like Earth Science, environmental sciences and engineering, or careers related to hazards, green tech or sustainability often need to be made more obvious – students often think that's where you go from science, without appreciating the role geography plays. There are even links and resources that suggest a range of bad ideas: Hesslewood (2023) describes how one of the options on Unifrog (a popular resource to support UCAS work) for geography is 'fence installation'.

There are lots of people 'doing geography' who didn't do a geography degree – and broadening participation and perceptions of the subject and community to include these is a key focus of the RGS strategy for 2030. This is particularly important at a time of global climate crisis: green and net-zero careers are increasingly vital to the UK's economy and providing satisfying and meaningful jobs for young people interested in the role they can play in the future.

Recent *Teaching Geography* articles from Hesslewood (2023) and Bytheway (2022) are excellent insights in to how to implement careers education and guidance in your geography curriculum and classroom planning, with downloads and resources to give examples. If you're looking for further inspiration, the RGS *Choose Geography* resources (https://www.rgs.org/choose-geography) are excellent and include:

- Resources, displays and materials you can use.
- Profiles of geographers and people working using geography.

- Great ideas about where and how to embed careers in your curriculum.
- Resources and suggestions for work experience opportunities in geography. It's worth noting that many are aimed at geography undergraduates rather than school-aged students!

One of the key conclusions from this chapter is the importance of teaching as a team sport. It's critical for your workload and wellbeing that you recognise – and accept – that it's not possible to do it all, and it's certainly not possible to do it all yourself. You need to know, understand and then use your school and community context to provide a sustainable outcome for your students. To do that, you need to make some tough decisions. You need to prioritise the things that are critical for your context or your students and make deliberate plans to manage some of the 'nice to have' items over time.

REFERENCES AND FURTHER READING

Adichie, C (2009) *The danger of a single story*, TED talk. Available at: https://www.youtube.com/watch?v=D9Ihs241zeg

Alcock, D. (2022) 'In praise of local fieldwork', *Teaching Geography*, 47 (1), 11–14.

Alcock, D. (2024) 'Grounds for hope in geography', *Teaching Geography*, 49 (1), 14–17.

Allison, S. & Tharby, A. (2015) *Making every lesson count*, Crown House.

Anderson, N. (2021) *Why do we need to decolonise geography?* Available at: https://decolonisegeography.com/blog/2021/02/why-do-we-need-to-decolonise-geography/

Anderson, N. et al. (2021) *Why the word 'slum' should not be used in geography classrooms*. Available at: https://decolonisegeography.com/blog/2021/08/why-the-word-slum-should-not-be-used-in-geography-classrooms/

Anderson, N. et al. (2022) 'Racial capitalism and the school geography curriculum', *Teaching Geography*, 47 (1), 15–18.

Bambrick-Santoyo, P. (2019, 2nd ed.) *Driven by data, 2.0: A practical guide to improve instruction*, Jossey-Bass.

Barton, R. and Finch Noyes, H. (2022) 'COP26: You choose – climate change', *Teaching Geography*, 47(1), 8–10.

Biddulph, M. (2017) 'Inclusive geographies: The illusion of inclusion', *Teaching Geography* 42 (2), 46–48.

Biddulph, M. et al. (2015) 'Values in school geography' in *Learning to teach geography in the secondary school. A companion to school experience* (3rd ed.), 279–286, Routledge.

Biddulph, M. et al. (2020) 'Inclusion' in *Learning to teach geography in the secondary school. A companion to school experience* (4th ed.), 128–153, Routledge.

Bishop, B. & Preece, D. (2024) 'Developing literacy across the geography curriculum using Scarborough's "reading rope"', *Teaching Geography*, 49 (1), 7–9.

Boxer, A. (2018) *Retrieval workload and pedagogical content knowledge*. Available at: https://achemicalorthodoxy.wordpress.com/2018/11/14/retrievalworkload-and-pedagogical-content-knowledge

Brace, S. (2024) 'Is your classroom plagued by "zombie resources"?' *TES Magazine*. Available at: https://www.tes.com/magazine/teaching-learning/secondary/the-problem-of-outdated-teaching-resources-schools-geography

Brace, S. & Souch, C. (2020) *Geography of Geography: The evidence base*, RGS. Available at: https://www.rgs.org/media/n2bdh5ng/geographyofgeographytheevidencebase.pdf

Burger, J. et al. (2023) 'Simulated climate solutions: Using the En-ROADS simulator', *Teaching Geography*, 48 (3), 114–116.

Bustin, R. (2018) 'What's your view? Curriculum ideologies and their impact in the Geography classroom', *Teaching Geography*, 43 (2) 61–63.

Bytheway, L. (2022) 'Future geographers: Careers as an integral part of the curriculum', *Teaching Geography*, 47 (3), 110–112.

Castree, N. et al. (2023) 'Exploring "power" as a concept in geographical education', *Teaching Geography*, 48 (3), 100–102.

Chandler, E. (2022) *Raising attainment in geography through Tier 2 vocabulary*, Available at: https://chandlergeog.wordpress.com/2022/02/19/raising-attainment-in-geography-through-tier-two-vocabulary/

Chandler, E. (2024) *Using a range of texts in the geography classroom*. Available at: https://chandlergeog.wordpress.com/2024/04/20/using-a-range-of-texts-in-the-geography-classroom/

Chiarella, D. & Vurro, G. (2020) 'Fieldwork and disability; An overview for an inclusive experience', *Geological Magazine,* 157 (11), 1933–1938. Available at: https://www.cambridge.org/core/journals/geological-magazine/article/fieldwork-and-disability-an-overview-for-an-inclusive-experience/4FDC4307FBA45729EA2F972E6C7C7C63

Chiles, M. (2021) *The feedback pendulum: A manifesto for enhancing feedback in education*, John Catt.

Cook (2010) 'Exploring students' personal experiences of geography fieldwork', *Teaching Geography*, 35 (2), 55–57.

Davies, O. (2020) 'Some simple ideas for running a geography club', *Teaching Geography*, 45 (3), 122–123.

Department for Education (2013) *National curriculum in England: geography programmes of study*. Available at: https://www.gov.uk/government/publications/national-curriculum-in-england-geography-programmes-of-study

Department for Education (2022) *Sustainability and climate change strategy.* Available at: https://www.gov.uk/government/publications/sustainability-and-climate-change-strategy

Dorling, D. (2019) 'Kindness: A new kind of rigour for British Geographers', *Emotion, Space and Society*, 33, 100630.

Draper, E. & Bailey, S. (2022) 'Improving understanding of geographical vocabulary at GCSE', *Teaching Geography*, 47 (3), 113–115.

Education Endowment Foundation (2021) *Effective professional development: Guidance report.* Available at: https://d2tic4wvo1iusb.cloudfront.net/production/eef-guidance-reports/effective-professional-development/EEF-Effective-Professional-Development-Guidance-Report.pdf

Enser, M. (2019) *Making every Geography lesson count*, Crown House.

Enser, M. (2021) *Powerful Geography*, Crown House.

Enser, Z. & Enser, M. (2020) *Fiorella & Meyer's generative learning in action*, John Catt.

Facer, J. (2016) *Teaching Vocabulary.* Available at: https://readingallthebooks.com/2016/07/02/teaching-vocabulary/

Faloyin, D. (2022) *Africa is Not A Country*, Harvill Secker.

Finn, M. (2022) 'Reading for a degree: Transitions to higher education', *Teaching Geography*, 47 (1), 36–39.

Fiorella, L. & Mayer, R. (2015) *Learning as a generative activity: Eight learning strategies that promote understanding.* Cambridge University Press.

Fry, W. (2018) 'Teaching controversial issues', *Teaching Geography*, 43 (3), 121–123.

Fryer, L. (2022) 'How to create a river fieldwork simulation in the classroom', *Teaching Geography*, 47 (2), 56–57.

Gardner (2022) *Planning your coherent 11–16 Geography curriculum: A design toolkit*, GA.

Geographical Association (2009) *A different view: A manifesto from the Geographical Association.* Available at: https://geography.org.uk/wp-content/uploads/2023/01/GA_ADVBookletFULL.pdf

Geographical Association (2023) *A framework for the school geography curriculum.* Available at: https://geography.org.uk/ga-curriculum-framework/

Geographical Association (2025) *Geography for everyone? Diversity, inclusion and the Geographical Association. A research report.* Available at: https://

geography.org.uk/wp-content/uploads/2025/02/Geography-for-Everyone-Diversity-and-Inclusion-2024.pdf

Geographical Association & Royal Geographical Society (2011) *The action plan for geography 2006–2011: Final report and evaluation*, GA & RGS. Available at: https://geography.org.uk/wp-content/uploads/2023/02/GA_APGFinalReportGARGSIBG.pdf

GL Assessment (2020) *Read all about it: Why reading is the key to GCSE success.* Available at: https://camdenlearning.org.uk/wp-content/uploads/2020/03/GL-Assessment.pdf

Graves, M. and Graves, B. (2003) *Scaffolding reading experiences: Designs for student success.* Christopher-Gordon Publishers, Inc.

Habib, B. (2023) 'Using authentic voices in the geography classroom through project-based learning', *Teaching Geography*, 48 (2), 64–67.

Hall, S. (1997) *Representation: Cultural representations and signifying practices*, Sage.

Hamill, A. (2020) *How GIS can add value to map work as a 'teach from the front' tool.* Available at: https://reflected857668995.wordpress.com/2020/10/20/how-gis-can-add-value-to-map-work-as-a-teach-from-the-front-tool/

Hamill, A. (2020a) *Doing virtual fieldwork with GIS* (webinar). Available at: https://www.youtube.com/watch?v=rvJ6Nf3eOYE

Hamill, A. (2020b) *How I designed a new biomes GIS task.* Available at: https://reflected857668995.wordpress.com/2020/08/30/how-i-designed-a-new-biomes-gis-task/

Hamill, A. (2021) 'Representing without misrepresenting: The ethics of case study writing', *Teaching Geography*, 46 (2), 53–55.

Hamill, A. (2021a) *Bringing landscapes to life – generative learning through field sketches.* Available at: https://reflected857668995.wordpress.com/2021/02/06/bringing-landscapes-to-life/

Hamill, A. (2023) 'Time for a seismic shift in teaching of plate tectonics?' *Teaching Geography*, 48 (2), 50–53.

Hamill, A. (2024) 'Taking field trips to the mantle', *Teaching Geography*, 49 (1), 10–13.

Hesslewood, A. (2021) 'Raising issues: where is the critical Geography in the school curriculum?', *Teaching Geography*, 46 (3), 109–111.

Hesslewood, A. (2023) 'Evaluating curriculum impact: using powerful disciplinary knowledge as "waypoints"', *Teaching Geography*, 48 (3), 107–110.

Hesslewood, A. (2023) 'Teaching about geography careers: from intent to impact', *Teaching Geography*, 48 (2), 61–63.

Hicks, D. (2019) 'Climate change: Bringing the pieces together', *Teaching Geography*, 44 (1), 20–23.

House of Commons Education & Skills Committee (2005) *Education outside the classroom: Second report of Session 2004–2005*. Available at: https://publications.parliament.uk/pa/cm200405/cmselect/cmeduski/120/120.pdf

Johnston, R. & Sidaway, J. (2016, 7th ed.) *Geography and geographers: Anglo-American human geography since 1945*, Routledge.

Jones, M. (2017) *The handbook of secondary geography*, GA.

Kearns, G. (2021a) 'Topple the racists 1: Decolonising the space and institutional memory of the university', *Geography*, 105 (3), 116–125.

Kearns, G. (2021b) 'Topple the racists 2: decolonising the space and institutional memory of geography', *Geography*, 106 (1), 4–15.

Kelman, I. (2020) *Disaster by Choice*, OUP.

Kitchen, R. & Maddison, J. (2021) 'A fieldwork toolkit for early career geography teachers', *Teaching Geography*, 46 (1), 17–20.

Kitchen, R. (2025) *High-quality geography fieldwork for all: a research report*, GA.

Knight, S. & Adger, N. (2015) 'Climate change – emerging scientific issues', *Teaching Geography*, 40 (3), 97–9.

Knight, S. (2013) 'Investigating weather through fieldwork', *Teaching Geography*, 38 (2), 72–74.

Lambert, D. & Balderstone, D. (2000, 2nd ed.) *Learning to Teach Geography in the Secondary School*, Routledge.

Lambert, D. & Jones, M. (2013) *Debates in geography education*, Routledge.

Lambert, D. & Morgan, J. (2010) *Teaching geography 11–18: A conceptual approach*, McGraw Hill.

Lambert, D. & Morgan, J. (2023) 'Geography education and racial literacy', *Teaching Geography*, 48 (3), 97–99

Lang, R. (2022) 'Supporting autistic students with fieldwork', *Teaching Geography*, 47 (3), 116–118.

Lazarus, R. (2009) 'Super wicked problems and climate change: Restraining the present to liberate the future', *Cornell Law Review*, 94, 1153–1234.

Lemov, D. (2021, 3rd ed.) *Teach like a champion 3.0: 63 techniques that put students on the path to college*, Jossey-Bass.

Levin, K. et al. (2012) 'Overcoming the tragedy of super wicked problems: Constraining our future selves to ameliorate global climate change', *Policy Sciences* 45, 123–152.

Levin, K. et al. (2007) 'Playing it forward: Path dependency, progressive incrementalism, and the "super wicked" problem of global climate change', IOP Conference Series Earth and Environmental Science 6 (50), DOI:10.1088/1755-1307/6/0/502002.

Livingstone, D. (1992) *The Geographical Tradition*, Blackwell.

Maddison, J. & Thurston, S. (2022) 'Supporting the mental health and wellbeing of learners during residential fieldwork', *Teaching Geography*, 47 (3), 106–109.

Mangal, M. (2020) 'Decolonising the curriculum: a case study', *Chartered College of Teaching Early Career Hub*. Available at: https://my.chartered.college/early-career-hub/decolonising-the-curriculum-a-case-study/

Marshall, T. (2016) *Prisoners of geography: Ten maps that tell you everything you need to know about global politics*, Elliott & Thompson Ltd.

Maude, A. (2016) 'What might powerful Geographical knowledge look like?', *Geography*, 101 (2).

Mayer (2020, 3rd edition) *Multimedia Learning*, Cambridge University Press.

McCrea, P. (2015) *Lean lesson planning: A practical approach to doing less and achieving more in the classroom*, CreateSpace.

McCrea, P. (2024) *Reverse design*. Available at: https://snacks.pepsmccrea.com/p/reverse-design

Meyer, J. and Land, R. (2003) 'Threshold concepts and troublesome knowledge: Linkages to ways of thinking and practising', 412–424 in C. Rust, *Improving student learning: Theory and practice ten years on*, Oxford Centre for Staff and Learning Development.

Milner, C. (2020) 'Classroom strategies for tackling the whiteness of geography', *Teaching Geography*, 45 (3), 105–107.

Milner, C. et al. (2021) 'How to start a conversation about diversity in education', *Teaching Geography*, 46 (2), 59–60.

Mitchell, D. (2013) 'What controls the "real" curriculum?', *Teaching Geography*, 38 (2), 60–62.

Mitchell, D (2022): 'GeoCapabilities 3: Knowledge and values in education for the Anthropocene', *International Research in Geographical and Environmental Education*, DOI: 10.1080/10382046.2022.2133353.

Myatt, M. (2016) *High challenge, low threat: How the best leaders find the balance*, John Catt.

Myatt, M. (2018) *The curriculum: Gallimaufrey to coherence*, John Catt.

McLean, D. et al. (2024) *Teacher Labour Market in England: Annual Report 2024*, National Foundation for Education Research. Available at: https://www.nfer.ac.uk/media/hqdglvra/teacher_labour_market_in_england_annual_report_2024.pdf

Ofsted (2021) *Subject Research review series: Geography*. Available at: https://www.gov.uk/government/publications/research-review-series-geography/research-review-series-geography

Ofsted (2023) *Getting our Bearings: Geography subject report*. Available at: https://www.gov.uk/government/publications/subject-report-series-geography/getting-our-bearings-geography-subject-report

Oracy Education Commission (2024) *We need to talk: The report of the Commission on the Future of Oracy Education in England*. Available at: https://oracyeducationcommission.co.uk/wp-content/uploads/2024/10/Future-of-Oracy-v23-web-13.pdf

Peppin, K. (2020) 'Getting outside! Investigating the school environment', *Teaching Geography*, 45 (2), 62–64.

Powell, C. (2023) 'Why drawing a diagram matters: Making the link with cognitive science', *Teaching Geography*, 48 (3), 111–113.

Preece, D. (2019) *Reflections: Baby steps with booklets*. Available at: https://drpreece.home.blog/2019/11/01/reflections-baby-steps-with-booklets/

Preece, D. (2019) *Making parents evening simple: Mail-merged information sheets*. Available at: https://drpreece.home.blog/2019/12/08/making-parents-evening-simple-mail-merged-information-sheets/

Preece, D. (2022) *Supporting geography candidates for university and Oxbridge: Introduction*. Available at: https://drpreece.home.blog/2022/07/10/supporting-geography-candidates-for-university-oxbridge-introduction/

Preece, D. & Tapsfield, A. (2023) *Recruitment in geography education: A crisis landscape*, GA. Available at: https://ga-blog.org/2023/08/10/recruitment-in-geography-education-a-crisis-landscape/

Puttick, S. & Murrey-Ndewa, A. (2020) 'Confronting the deafening silence on race in geography education in England: Learning from anti-racist, decolonial and Black geographies', *Geography*, 105 (3), 126–134.

Rackley, K. (2018) 'How to develop independent investigation questioning skills at home', *Teaching Geography*, 42 (1), 11–12.

Rackley, K. (2019) 'Resources to teach the changing nature of climate and energy', *Teaching Geography*, 44 (2) 62–65.

Rackley, K. (2020) 'Climate change – a safeguarding issue?' *GA Magazine*, 46, 20–21.

Rackley, K. (2022) 'Fostering empathy in the teaching of natural hazards', *Teaching Geography*, 47 (2), 67–69.

Rawling, E. (2007) *Planning and developing the curriculum*, GTIP Think Piece, GA. Available at: https://geography.org.uk/wp-content/uploads/2023/05/GTIP_planningcurriculum.pdf

Rawling, E. (2008) 'Planning your key stage 3 curriculum', *Teaching Geography*, 33 (3), 114–119.

Rawling, E. (2016) 'The geography curriculum 5-19: What does it all mean?', Teaching Geography, 41 (1), 6–9.

Rawlings Smith, E. & Kinder, A. (2023) *The professional needs and views of teachers of geography: A national research report by the Geographical Association*, GA. Available at: https://geography.org.uk/wp-content/uploads/2023/02/GA_National_Research_Report_2023.pdf

Reilly, S. (2022) 'Supporting trainee teachers to decolonise the school geography curriculum', *Teaching Geography*, 47 (2), 64–66.

Rittel, H. & Webber, M. (1973) 'Dilemmas in a General Theory of Planning', *Policy Sciences*, 4(2), 155–169.

Roberts, M. (2011) *What makes a geography lesson good?* GA. Available at: https://geography.org.uk/wp-content/uploads/2023/01/GA_ITE_TE_What_makes_a_geography_lesson_good_ED.pdf.

Roberts, M. (2021) *Geographical enquiry and practice: GA curriculum framework advisory group report*, unpublished.

Roberts, M. (2023, 2nd ed.) *Geography through enquiry*, GA.

Roediger, H. & Karpicke, J. (2006) 'Test-enhanced learning: Taking memory tests improves long-term retention', *Psychological Science*, 17 (3), 249–255.

Rosling, H. (2006) *The best stats you've ever seen*, TED Talk. Available at: https://www.ted.com/talks/hans_rosling_the_best_stats_you_ve_ever_seen

Rosling, H. (2009) *Let my dataset change your mindset*, TED Talk, Available at: https://www.ted.com/talks/hans_rosling_let_my_dataset_change_your_mindset

Rosling, H. (2014) How not to be ignorant about the world, TED Talk, Available at: https://www.ted.com/talks/hans_and_ola_rosling_how_not_to_be_ignorant_about_the_world

Rosling (2019) *Factfulness: Ten reasons we're wrong about the world – and why things are better than you think*, Sceptre.

Royal Geographical Society (2021) *'I didn't have any teachers that looked like me': Sharing the experience of Black, Asian and minority ethnic geography teachers*, research report. Available at: https://www.rgs.org/about-us/what-is-geography/geography-in-schools/i-didnt-have-any-teachers-that-looked-like-me

Sammar, I. (2024) 'Decolonial and anti-racist pedagogy through personal geographies', *Teaching Geography*, 49 (1), 22–25.

Scarborough, H. (2001) 'Connecting early language and literacy to later reading (dis)abilities: Evidence, theory, and practice', 97–110 in S. Neuman & D. Dickinson, *Handbook for research in early literacy*, Guilford Press.

Searl, C. (2021a) *Methods of collecting fieldwork data*, GA.

Searl, C. (2021b) *Methods of presenting fieldwork data*, GA.

Searl, C. (2021c) *Methods of analysing fieldwork data*, GA.

Sheriff, F. (2024) *100 Ideas for secondary teachers: Geography fieldwork*, Bloomsbury.

Sherrington, T. (2017) *The learning rainforest*, John Catt.

Sherrington, T. (2019) *Rosenshine's principles in action*, John Catt.

Siegel, L. et al. (2025) *En-ROADS technical reference*. Available at https://docs.climateinteractive.org/projects/en-roads-reference-guide/en/latest/

Sinclair, D. & de Fonseka, A. (2022) 'Operationalising anti-racist pedagogy in a secondary geography classroom', *Teaching Geography*, 47 (2), 58–60.

Sinclair, D. (2022) 'Pedagogies for diverse classrooms: why should geography matter to me?' *Teaching Geography*, 47 (3), 102–104.

Sloggett, G. (2021) 'Covid-19: an opportunity to review fieldwork provision', *Teaching Geography*, 46 (1), 29–31.

Snelling, J. (2015) 'Fieldwork on your CV', *Teaching Geography*, 40 (3) 124.

Stockings, K. (2023a) *Teaching geography through books (Part 1)*. Available at: https://www.katestockings.com/geographycurriculum/teaching-geography-through-books

Stockings, K. (2023b) *Teaching geography through books (Part 2)*. Available at: https://www.katestockings.com/geographycurriculum/teaching-geography-through-books-part-2

Tayler, L. (2024) *Visualising physical geography*, Routledge.

Tharby, A. (2018) *How to explain absolutely anything to absolutely anyone: The art & science of teacher explanation*, Crown House.

Walshe, N. & Perry, J. (2022) 'Transformative geography education: developing eco-capabilities for a flourishing and sustainable future', *Teaching Geography*, 47 (3), 94–97.

Walshe, N. (2017) 'Literacy', 198–211 in M. Jones, *The handbook of secondary geography*, GA.

Webb, H. (2025) *Learning to support physical geography for non-specialists*. Available at: https://teachingphysicalgeog.wordpress.com/2025/01/21/help-im-a-human-geographer-get-me-out-of-here/

Weeden, P. (2005) 'Feedback in the geography classroom: Developing the use of assessment for learning', *Teaching Geography*, 30 (3) 161–163.

Weeden, P. (2013) 'How do we link assessment to making progress in geography?', in D. Lambert & M. Jones, *Debates in geography education*, Routledge.

Weeden, P. (2017) 'Assessing Geography', 182–197 in M. Jones, *The handbook of secondary geography*, GA.

World Health Organisation (2021) *World health statistics 2021: Monitoring health for the SDGs*, WHO. Available at: https://iris.who.int/bitstream/handle/10665/342703/9789240027053-eng.pdf

Wiggins, G. & McTighe, J. (2005, 2nd ed.) *Understanding by Design*, ASCD.

Wilingham, D. (2021, 2nd ed.) *Why Don't Students Like School?*, Jossey-Bass.

Wood, Z. & Walker, J. (2007) 'Learning outside the classroom: what can be done in lesson time?', *Teaching Geography*, 32 (3) 135–138.

Young, M. & Lambert, D. (2014) *Knowledge and the future school: Curriculum and social justice*, Bloomsbury.

Young, M. & Muller, J. (2010) 'Three educational scenarios for the future: Lessons from the sociology of knowledge', *European Journal of Education*, 45(1), 11–27.

Young, M. (2008) *Bringing knowledge back in: From social constructivism to social realism in the sociology of education*, Routledge.